THOMAS HOWARD MOORE III
329 MAIN STREET, APT 1A
P.O. BOX 22
BINGHAM, MAINE 04920-0022
UNITED STATES OF AMERICA

2013

from Patricia J. Moore

DREAM DESTINATIONS

DREAM DESTINATIONS

THE WORLD'S MOST UNFORGETTABLE PLACES

MARY-ANN GALLAGHER

METRO BOOKS
NEW YORK

CONTENTS

Introduction.. 6
Giant's Causeway, Northern Ireland................... 8
Stonehenge, England.................................... 10
Alhambra, Granada, Spain............................. 14
Barcelona, Catalunya, Spain........................... 18
Mont-St-Michel, Normandy, France.................. 22
Loire Valley, Central France........................... 26
Paris, Northern France................................. 30
Bruges, West Flanders, Belgiu........................ 34

Neuschwanstein, Bavaria, Germany.................. 38
Hammerfest, Finnmark, Norway...................... 40
Rome, Central Italy...................................... 42
Venice, Veneto, Italy.................................... 46
Metéora, Thessaly, Greece............................. 50
St Petersburg, Northwestern Russia................. 52
Cappadocia, Central Anatolia, Turkey............... 56
Petra, Arabah, Jordan................................... 58
Aswan to Luxor, Southern Egypt..................... 62

Skeleton Coast, Northern Namibia.................... 66
Victoria Falls, Zambia–Zimbabwe Border........... 68
Samarkand, Central Uzbekistan....................... 72
Taj Mahal, Agra, India.................................. 76
Darjeeling Railway, West Bengal, India.............. 80
Angkor Wat, Siem Reap, Cambodia.................. 84
Borobudur, Java, Indonesia............................ 88
Great Wall, Northern China............................. 92
Forbidden City, Beijing, China......................... 96

34 Bruges
188 Haukadalur
10 Stonehenge
8 Giant's Causeway
30 Paris
22 Mont-St-Michel
26 Loire Valley
14 Alhambra
18 Barcelona

124 Banff
128 Churchill
146 New England
134 Yellowstone
142 Washington Monuments
120 Vancouver
132 Monument Valley
138 Everglades
154 Chichén Itzá
158 Old Havana
150 Mexican Day of the Dead
162 Costa Rican Cloud Forest
180 Manaus and the Amazon
166 Galápagos
170 Inca Trail
184 Iguaçu Falls
116 Rapa Nui
178 Perito Moreno Glacier
174 Tierra del Fuego

Kyoto, Honshu, Japan... 100
Uluru, Northern Territory, Australia.....................104
Great Barrier Reef, Queensland, Australia............108
Tasmanian Wilderness, Australia.........................112
Rapa Nui, Chile...116
Vancouver, British Columbia, Canada..................120
Banff, Alberta, Canada... 124
Churchill, Manitoba, Canada.................................128
Monument Valley, Utah, United States.................132

Yellowstone, Western United States.....................134
Everglades, Florida, United States....................... 138
Washington Monuments, United States...............142
New England, Northeastern United States..........146
Mexican Day of the Dead.......................................150
Chichén Itzá, Yucatán Peninsula, Mexico............ 154
Old Havana, Northwestern Cuba.......................... 158
Cloud Forest, Costa Rica....................................... 162
Galápagos, Ecuador..166

Inca Trail, Near Cuzco, Peru..................................170
Tierra del Fuego, Argentina and Chile...................174
Perito Moreno Glacier, Argentina..........................178
Manaus and the Amazon, Brazil............................180
Iguaçu Falls, Brazil–Argentina Border...................184
Haukadalur, Southern Iceland................................188

Index...190
Acknowledgements..192

40 Hammerfest

52 St Petersburg

38 Neuschwanstein

92 Great Wall

46 Venice

56 Cappadocia

50 Metéora

72 Samarkand

96 Forbidden City

42 Rome

58 Petra

76 Taj Mahal

100 Kyoto

62 Aswan to Luxor

80 Darjeeling Railway

84 Angkor Wat

88 Borobudur

108 Great Barrier Reef

68 Victoria Falls

104 Uluru

66 Skeleton Coast

112 Tasmanian Wilderness

INTRODUCTION

This book contains 50 of the most extraordinary sights to be found on Earth, many of which have been recognized by UNESCO for their outstanding natural or cultural significance. The destinations are scattered across the globe, from the world's northernmost city, where the Northern Lights dance across the winter sky, to Argentina's Tierra del Fuego, at the very end of the world.

Among the oldest manmade sites included in these pages are the prehistoric stone circle at Stonehenge, which has stood on the vast plain of Salisbury for more than 5,000 years, and the startling rose-red city of Petra, etched into the sandstone walls of a desert canyon about two millennia ago. Even older are the ruins at Thebes (modern Aswan), the capital of ancient Egypt during the New Kingdom, erected near the banks of the great River Nile from the 16th century BC.

Other destinations showcase the architecture of a particular era. In Rome, the staggering ruins of the Colosseum and the Pantheon are testament to the power and wealth of one of Europe's greatest ancient civilizations. The superb Gothic churches and squares of Bruges vividly recall the city's Golden Age during the Middle Ages, when it was one of the most important trading centres in Europe. Venice, a ravishing island city, has changed little since its sumptuous Renaissance palaces were erected along the Grand Canal. Barcelona boasts Europe's largest and most complete Gothic quarter, but is best known for its fairytale Modernista architecture, particularly the daring constructions of visionary architect Antoni Gaudí. The beautiful Loire Valley, south of Paris, is scattered with opulent châteaux, built for the kings and courtiers of Renaissance France. Cuba's atmospheric capital, Havana, is replete with the elegant colonial architecture imported by its first Spanish

rulers. And among the modern cities included in our list is Vancouver, with its cluster of skyscrapers backed by stunning mountain scenery.

Also included here are spectacular sites erected by remarkable civilizations that have since waned or even disappeared. These splendid constructions can raise more questions than they answer. Among them, for example, is the lofty city of Machu Picchu, set high in the Peruvian Andes. Probably built during the mid-15th century, the site's exact function remains a mystery. Was it a winter palace complex for the Inca rulers, or was it a place of worship and devotion to the Inca deities? Even more mysterious are the huge stone figures that are scattered across the remote Pacific island of Rapa Nui, also known as Easter Island. Very little is known about the vanished people who erected these stylized sculptures, and their purpose, although apparently religious, remains a matter of conjecture. Considerably more is known about the Khmer empire, which ruled a large swathe of Indochina from the 9th to the 13th centuries, and bequeathed the enormous temple of Angkor Wat, in modern Cambodia. This breathtaking complex is a symbolic representation of the sacred mountain of Meru, abode of the Hindu gods and centre of the universe. Similarly, the builders of Borobudur, on the Indonesian island of Java, sought to embody a spiritual concept when they created the vast pyramid-shaped temple. The journey through the gigantic temple – the largest in the world – constitutes a spiritual pilgrimage through the three most important realms of Buddhist cosmology, culminating in the lofty stupa pointing towards Nirvana.

Many of the great monuments described on these pages have a spiritual function. Some of the beautiful wooden temples and shrines found in the ancient Japanese capital of Kyoto have existed here since the eighth century AD, when the city was founded. They are particularly beautiful during *hanami*, the celebrated Japanese cherry-blossom viewing season, when they emerge from a cloud of pale pink petals. The city of Samarkand, an important hub on the Silk Route, preserves some exceptionally fine Islamic architecture, particularly in the Registan. This, the city's most impressive square, is overlooked by three immense madrassahs, covered with dazzling, gilded mosaics. Kukulkan, the plumed serpent, was the most important deity for the Maya people of Chichén Itzá, a vast stone city on the Yucatán peninsula. Kukulkan is honoured by an enormous stepped temple, built between the 10th and 13th centuries and carefully aligned according to astonishingly advanced astronomical guidelines. Thanks to these exact alignments, every year, on the spring and autumn equinoxes, a shadow is cast that creates the illusion of a gigantic, feathered snake slithering down the staircase. In France, as the Maya were building their great temple, a magnificent abbey was being constructed on a lonely islet off the coast of Normandy. Dedicated to the fiery archangel, whose statue adorns the highest spire, the Abbey of Mont-St-Michel has become one of the country's most important attractions. On the other side of the world, in the heart of Australia, Uluru (formerly called Ayers Rock) holds a special, spiritual significance for the indigenous people who have dwelt in the region for more than 40,000 years.

The natural wonders of the world are celebrated here too. From geysers to volcanoes, mountains to waterfalls, rainforest to deserts, we describe the Earth's glorious natural treasures. Among them are the unique wetlands of the Everglades, with its abundant wildlife and fascinating ecosystems; the eerie Northern Lights which swirl through the night sky in the frozen north; and the cloud forests of Costa Rica, which boast a greater biodiversity than the whole of Europe or North America. Just as staggering is the sheer abundance of endemic flora and fauna on the Galápagos Islands, where Darwin began to formulate his theory of evolution by natural selection, revolutionizing scientific and philosophical beliefs. In the geological hotspots of Iceland and Yellowstone, geysers spout great jets of steam and fumaroles sputter, and, in the vast icefields of Patagonia, the Perito Moreno Glacier advances slowly across a lake before shattering with a thunderous crash. On the borders of Zambia and Zimbabwe, the Zambezi River cascades into the Victoria Falls, one of the largest and most powerful waterfalls anywhere in the world. Its beauty is only matched by the Iguaçu Falls, a breathtaking cascade that is

formed by almost 300 smaller cataracts. The sheer theatricality of nature is also celebrated in Northern Ireland, where an enormous patchwork of basalt columns is evocatively called the 'Giant's Causeway', due to the once held belief that it was the work of giants. There are underwater marvels to be discovered, too, most notably in the Great Barrier Reef, a 3,000-kilometre-long (1,900-mile) coral reef system off the northwestern coast of Australia. Here the water teems with hundreds of species of aquatic creatures, including turtles, sharks and manatees. The world's largest land mammal, the polar bear, has become the symbol of the remote Canadian town of Churchill. Hundreds of polar bears converge on the tiny town as winter approaches, hungrily waiting for the ice to freeze over on Hudson Bay to aid them in their hunt for seals, their primary food source.

In the 21st century, few places in the world remain entirely unspoilt by man. Some of these last remaining wildernesses are celebrated here, including the mist-swathed dunes of Namibia's Skeleton Coast, where the sun-dried bones of beached whales and shipwrecks litter the treacherous coastline. There are vast tracts of the Amazon rainforest that have yet to be mapped, and where entire peoples still live without any contact with the outside world. In Tasmania, a huge tract of the island has been protected by UNESCO as the Tasmanian Wilderness Area. This region offers some of the finest hiking to be found anywhere, including the justly celebrated Overland Track.

The Overland Track is just one of the marvellous trails included in this selection of dream destinations. Other famous journeys include the Inca Trail, a spectacular hike through the Peruvian Andes that culminates with the spellbinding city of Machu Picchu. The Wilderness Waterway is a week-long canoe trail through the unique watery landscape of the Everglades in southern Florida. And, in Egypt, the simple, white-sailed feluccas continue to journey down the Nile from Aswan to Luxor much as they have done for millennia. In India, the enchanting 'Toy Railway' makes its excruciatingly steep ascent from the sweltering plains to the lofty hill station of Darjeeling, 2,128 metres (6,980 ft) above sea level, and overlooked by the mighty peaks of the Himalayas. And the Great Wall of China, which unfurls for thousands of kilometres through the mountains, ravines and deserts of northern China, offers the opportunity to hike along the world's largest manmade monument.

Mary-Ann Gallagher

GIANT'S CAUSEWAY

Giant's Causeway
NORTHERN
IRELAND

Latitude 55°14'N **Longitude** 6°30'W

Location County Antrim, Northern Ireland

Formed 60 million years ago

Materials Basalt

Approximate area 4 million square metres
(43 million sq ft)

Approximate dimensions 12 metres (40 ft)
high and 28 metres (92 ft) thick in places

'When the world was moulded and fashioned out of
formless chaos, this must have been the bit over – a
remnant of chaos,' wrote Thackeray in 1842, after visiting
the famous Giant's Causeway (*Clochán na bhFómharachon*
in Irish) off Northern Ireland's dramatic northeastern
coast. Seabirds wheel over jagged cliffs and waves dash
against the basalt columns, so neatly arranged that their
curious forms have long evoked legends of giants.

The most famous of these stories features the great Irish
hero and giant Fionn MacCumhaill (Finn McCool). He
began to build the causeway in order to reach his enemy, a
fierce Scottish giant called Benandonner, who lived on an
island just off the Scottish coast. Although myths of giants
seem curiously credible in this otherworldly landscape,
the causeway was actually formed by a furious volcanic
explosion 60 million years ago, which threw up spurts of
red-hot lava. The lava solidified over millennia into the
dark grey basalt columns, with their characteristic
hexagonal shape, which form the strange patchwork puzzle
of the Giant's Causeway today.

The site was 'discovered' in 1693, and triggered a heated
debate between academics and naturalists: had this
apparently unique phenomenon been created by the
elements or carved out by humans? It wasn't until 1771
that a French scientist proved its volcanic origins. Now a
UNESCO World Heritage Site and a protected nature
reserve, the causeway is the most popular visitor attraction
in Northern Ireland.

The basalt columns of the Giant's Causeway appear to have been arranged so carefully that it is hardly surprising that people believed it had been built by giants – right up until the late 18th century.

TRAVELLER'S TIPS

Best time to go: Visit at low tide, when more of the causeway is on display: early morning or late afternoon. There are also fewer tourists at these times.

Look out for: The basalt columns moulded into fanciful forms. such as the Wishing Chair. Camel and Harp.

Dos and don'ts: Do leave time to walk one of several superb walking trails. with possible sightings of seabirds including petrels, cormorants. shags and wagtails.

STONEHENGE

ENGLAND

Stonehenge

Latitude 51°10'N **Longitude** 1°49'W

Location Salisbury Plain, England, UK

Built c. 3000–1500 BC

Materials Stone

Approximate area 1,200 square metres (13,000 sq ft)

Approximate dimensions The diameter of the outer stone circle is 39.5 metres (130 ft)

The ancient stone circle at Stonehenge is perhaps the most iconic prehistoric monument anywhere in the world. And yet, despite its fame, this enigmatic structure is still shrouded in mystery, and almost nothing is known about the shadowy people who arranged the massive stones.

Although theories about the site's age and function abound, most academics agree on a rough timescale. It is generally agreed that Stonehenge was built in three stages, although it was probably an important cult site for about 4,000 years before the first structures were erected. Around 3000 BC, the

henge (a circular bank-and-ditch enclosure) was dug into the chalky soil of Salisbury Plain, a flat expanse in southwest modern-day England. A century or so later, a timber structure was erected on the site, but the wood, of course, has long rotted and nothing survives. In the second (and most important) stage, around 2500 BC, the first stones were brought to the site and arranged in circular patterns. The earliest of these were the celebrated bluestones, each weighing about four tons, which were brought from the Preseli Hills in Wales, about 400 kilometres (249 miles) away. When wet, these stones seem to turn a delicate shade of blue, which gives

The enigmatic stone circle continues to perplex archaeologists. Was it a place of worship, a calendar in stone – or something else altogether?

them their name. Later, in the third stage, the even larger sarsen stones were brought to the site to form an outer ring; arranged in pairs and topped with lintels, they still provide Stonehenge with its instantly recognizable silhouette. Inside this ring, the builders placed five pairs of still-larger stones in a horseshoe shape. The arrangement of the stones was later modified, when a part of the bluestone circle was removed and

TRAVELLER'S TIPS

Best time to go: Stonehenge attracts about 900,000 tourists annually. Visit as early or late in the day as possible to see the stones at their most photogenic.

Look out for: Note how the outer stones have been shaped so that they are wider at the top, to ensure a constant perspective when viewed from the ground.

Dos and don'ts: If it's a fine day, do bring a picnic. There are no restaurant

The most ambitious phase of the construction at Stonehenge was the erection of the outer stone circle. Thirty vertical sarsen stones were used, each estimated to weigh up to 50 tons, while another 30 stones were hoisted up to form the horizontal lintels. Some stones were carved with daggers, axes and other devices.

the remaining stones in the circle were repositioned. It is believed that the site fell out of use during the second millennium BC.

Stonehenge was clearly an important ceremonial structure, but its precise function remains a mystery. Some believe that it is a kind of astronomical calculator, and point to the precise alignment of the stones with the sun and the moon. Recent studies have led to a new theory linking Stonehenge with Durrington Walls, the largest henge in Britain, found three kilometres (2 miles) north of Stonehenge itself. It has been suggested that the two sites are interlinked: Durrington Walls, with its rings of enormous wooden posts, represented the living world, while Stonehenge, where the circles were made of immutable stone, represented the realm of the dead. The cremated human remains found at Stonehenge are, according to this theory, possibly members of an elite, or even a ruling dynasty. This theory has been given substance.

It was long believed that Stonehenge functioned as a burial site only for a small part of its history (roughly concurrent with the introduction of the standing stones), but carbon dating has proved that burials have taken place at Stonehenge from its earliest incarnation. The high number of burials has led some academics to suggest that the site may have functioned as a healing sanctuary, a sort of ancient precursor of Lourdes. The discovery of the Amesbury Archer, buried around 2300 BC, may have lent weight to this theory. Isotope testing on the skeleton's teeth proved the Archer came from the Alps, and that he was afflicted with a crippling injury in one leg.

Although Stonehenge was probably composed of inner and outer stone circles, this cannot be proved. Only about half of the stones survive in situ, and many of the assumed stone sockets have never been found.

ALHAMBRA

Latitude 37°10'N **Longitude** 03°35'W

Location Granada, Spain

Built From 1238

Materials Wood, stone, stucco and tile

Approximate area 142,000 square metres
(1,528,000 sq ft)

Approximate dimensions 740 x 205 x 25 metres
(2,427 x 672 x 82 ft)

The spellbinding Alhambra, the great fortress and palace which gazes out over Granada, embodies the spirit of old Al-Andalus like nowhere else in Spain. To dawdle in its intricately stuccoed chambers, or amble through the perfumed gardens, is to return to the heady years of the 14th century, when Granada, the last surviving Muslim kingdom in Spain, was still ruled by the Nasrid dynasty.

It was under the last Nasrid rulers, Yusuf I (1333–53) and his son, Muhammed V (1353–91), that the Alhambra was transformed from a fortified citadel into a gracious palace-city.

The name comes from the Arabic Al Qal'at al-Hamra, meaning 'the red fortress', in reference to the red clay used in the original construction; the name was retained, even after the new palace was painted a dazzling white. The new Alhambra was designed to represent 'paradise on Earth', with a series of refined palaces, gardens filled with tinkling fountains, bath-houses, and a canal ('the Sultan's Canal') to provide it with a constant supply of water. Even the presence of the snowcapped peaks of the Sierra Nevada mountain range, forming a spectacular backdrop, were integrated into the plans for the new palace-city. Most of the earlier fortress was

At dusk, the setting sun imbues the Alhambra with a rosy glow that recalls the origins of its name 'the red fortress'.

demolished to make way for the Alhambra, but a sturdy watchtower (Torre de la Vela) still occupies the northwestern end of the complex, and offers superb views over the city below.

The Nasrid Palace (actually a series of interconnected palaces) is the soul of the Alhambra, exquisitely decorated by the finest artists of the age. Although subsequent Christian rulers

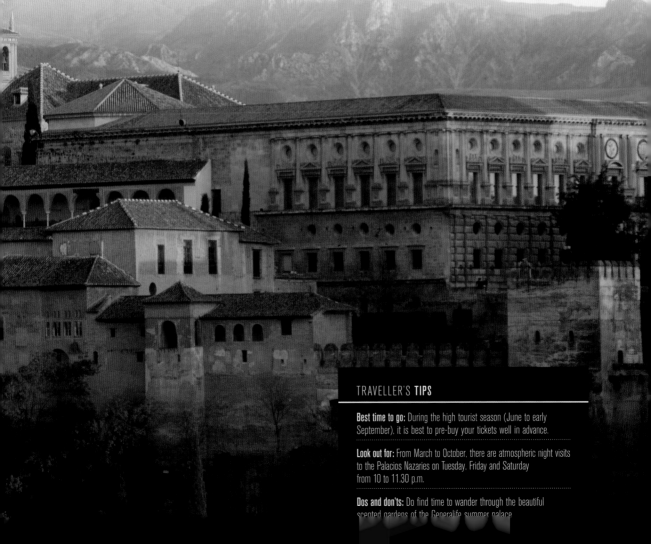

TRAVELLER'S TIPS

Best time to go: During the high tourist season (June to early September), it is best to pre-buy your tickets well in advance.

Look out for: From March to October, there are atmospheric night visits to the Palacios Nazaries on Tuesday, Friday and Saturday from 10 to 11.30 p.m.

Dos and don'ts: Do find time to wander through the beautiful scented gardens of the Generalife summer palace

The Generalife, which was designed as a summer palace, is at the eastern end of the Alhambra complex. Its scented gardens are magical, filled with birdsong and gurgling fountains. The gardens are arranged on terraces and frame views of Granada's whitewashed Arabic quarter, the Albaicín, which spills down the hillside below.

(Granada fell to Ferdinand and Isabella, the 'Catholic Kings', in 1492) clumsily remodelled or even demolished parts of the palace, it remains the most substantially intact Muslim palace anywhere in the world. The humble materials used to create this marvellous vision – wood, stucco and tile – symbolize the ephemeral nature of life on Earth, but the exquisite craftsmanship with which they have been sculpted rend hommage to the eternal glory of God. Water is everywhere: in the limpid pools designed to reflect the graceful arabesques of the stucco arches, and in the burble of cooling fountains.

Among the finest of the Alhambra's numerous chambers and patios is the Patio de los Arrayanes (Court of the Myrtles), found near the entrance to the palace. Its centrepiece is a long, tiled pool, fringed with myrtle hedges and overlooked by intricately sculpted stucco arcades. The grandest patio of all is the Patio de los Leones (Court of the Lions), in the very centre of the palace, which was designed to represent the Garden of Paradise. The rectangular patio is divided into four sections, representing the four corners of Paradise according to Islamic tradition, and each watered by a symbolic 'river'. The chambers off this patio are the most opulent, with lavish decoration which includes extravagant muquarnas ceilings; the finest of these can be found in the Sala de las Dos Hermanas (Chamber of the Two Sisters) and the Sala de los Abecerrajes (Chamber of the Abecerrajes; named for a family supposedly slaughtered here in 1492). The Sala de los Reyes (Chamber of the Kings), a banqueting room just off the Patio de los Leones, boasts a unique frescoed ceiling depicting several 14th-century rulers of Granada, which was painted on leather panels.

At the centre of the Patio de los Leones stands the fountain that gives the court its name, adorned with 12 stylized lions. The court is flanked on all sides by a gallery supported with slender columns of white marble.

BARCELONA

Latitude 41°23'N **Longitude** 2°11'E

Location Catalunya, Spain

Population 1,615,900, with 3,186,400 in Greater Barcelona

Approximate area 101 square kilometres (39 sq miles)

Official languages Catalan and Spanish

Currency The euro

Spain's most flamboyant city lies on the Mediterranean coast, fringed with beaches on one side and undulating hills on the other. At its heart is Europe's largest Gothic Quarter, a warren of narrow alleys and secret squares. Beyond this stretches the Eixample, the 19th-century extension to the city's medieval core, which contains the finest collection of Modernista monuments in the world. The most extravagant Modernista buildings came from the imagination of one man, Antoni Gaudí, whose fairytale spires for the great temple of the Sagrada Família remain the city's most emblematic landmark.

Barcelona is the capital of Catalunya, once a powerful kingdom in its own right. The region still retains its own language, customs, cuisine and a unique heritage that shares very little with mainstream Spanish culture. You'll hear Catalan spoken more often than Spanish, and all road signs are written in the local language. Madrid may be the Spanish capital, but Barcelona likes to think of itself as the front-runner when it comes to style, design and culture. The city was transformed for the 1992 Olympic Games, and its love of modern design continues unabated. From Ricardo Bofill's billowing design for the Hotel Vela (2009) overlooking the port, to Jean Nouvel's conical, multi-hued tower, the Torre Agbar (2004), Barcelona remains committed to showcasing bold, dynamic architecture.

TRAVELLER'S **TIPS**

Best time to go: Barcelona is popular year-round thanks to its mild. Mediterranean climate. May and June are lovely, when the gardens are in bloom.

Look out for: Chocolate. Barcelona has had a heady reputation for its chocolate-makers since the cocoa bean was first introduced to the Old World.

Dos and don'ts: Do remember that you are in Catalunya. which has a distinct language and culture from the rest of Spain.

The celebrated avenue of La Rambla slices through the tightly packed heart of old Barcelona. It is lined with kiosks selling everything from flowers to canaries.

The Plaça Reial, in the Gothic Quarter, is an elegant 19th-century square, with a graceful fountain and a pair of very ornate lamp-posts designed by the young Antoni Gaudí. It is packed with lively cafés and restaurants, which set out their tables on the square throughout the year.

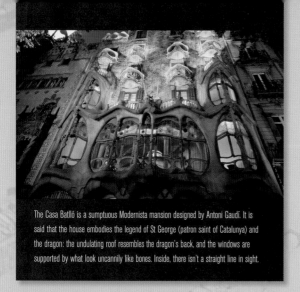

The Casa Batlló is a sumptuous Modernista mansion designed by Antoni Gaudí. It is said that the house embodies the legend of St George (patron saint of Catalunya) and the dragon: the undulating roof resembles the dragon's back, and the windows are supported by what look uncannily like bones. Inside, there isn't a straight line in sight.

The magnificent Gothic Quarter (Barri Gòtic) bears witness to the city's Golden Age of the 13th to 15th centuries. The Basilica de Santa Maria del Mar, an exquisite 14th-century church, reveals the wealth of the medieval merchants whose maritime trade made the city's fortune. Their handsome Gothic mansions, complete with graceful stone courtyards and sweeping staircases, still line nearby Carrer Montcada. (Five of them have been remodelled to contain the celebrated Picasso Museum.) The quarter is dominated by the soaring spires of the cathedral of La Seu, largely built between the 13th and 15th centuries over the ruins of a Visigothic basilica.

Once Catalunya became part of the burgeoning nation of Spain with the marriage of Ferdinand and Isabella in 1469, its fortunes waned as power became concentrated in Castille. It wasn't until the 19th century that business boomed once again, and Barcelona began to expand. The new extension, called the Eixample, was constructed with wide, airy boulevards and elegant mansions. The wealthy commissioned the finest architects of the day to build their homes, and the Eixample became a showcase of Modernista architecture. Catalan Modernism, which had some similarities with French Art Nouveau and other fin-de-siècle architectural styles, was characterized by curving lines, organic forms and lavish detail. The greatest exponents of the style were Puig i Cadafalch, Domènech i Montaner and, most famous of all, Antoni Gaudí. His surreal imagination has left its imprint across the city, in extraordinary buildings like La Pedrera apartment building, which resembles a cream puff, or the glorious Park Güell, with its fanciful pavilions and sinuous mosaic bench.

Most famous of all Antoni Gaudí's creations is the Sagrada Família, the enormous (as yet unfinished) temple topped by its signature bulbous spires, which is visible from almost anywhere in the city.

MONT-ST-MICHEL

Latitude 48°38'N **Longitude** 01°30'W

Location Normandy, France

Built Abbey constructed from AD 708

Materials Granite, limestone and marble

Approximate area Island covers 958,000 square metres (10 million sq ft)

Approximate dimensions Island is 1,000 x 960 x 80 metres (3,280 x 3,150 x 260 ft)

Mont-St-Michel

FRANCE

A lonely islet surrounded by vast, shifting sandbanks, Mont-St-Michel is crowned by the soaring silhouette of an immense medieval abbey. The abbey, like the islet, is dedicated to the archangel St Michael, whose statue floats high above the church.

The islet, a conical granite outcrop just off the Normandy coast, was once linked to the mainland by a narrow land bridge that appeared only at low tide. According to legend, St Michael appeared in a vision to St Aubert, bishop of nearby Avranches, in AD 708 and asked him to construct an oratory on the islet. But Aubert ignored the vision, until finally the

wrathful St Michael pointed a fiery finger at him and bored a hole in the bishop's head. (His pierced skull is still displayed in an elaborate reliquary in the basilica of Avranches.)

St Aubert commissioned the first oratory in the eighth century, although almost nothing of this early building has survived. A community of Benedictine monks came to the island in AD 966, when the church buildings were enlarged. The Romanesque edifice begun during the tenth century is still the kernel of the abbey complex, but the most beautiful buildings were erected during the 13th century in the Gothic style.

UNESCO designated Mont-St-Michel as a World Heritage site in 1979, and it now attracts more than three million visitors a year.

This section of the abbey is still known as La Merveille (The Marvel) and incorporates the magnificent refectory and cloister as well as some lavish apartments, all daringly built on three tiers on the islet's steep flanks. La Merveille was paid for by Philippe II of France (1165–1223), who was filled with remorse at the damage caused to the abbey during his unsuccessful attempts to capture the mont in 1203.

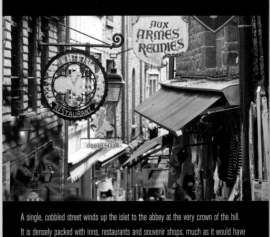

A single, cobbled street winds up the islet to the abbey at the very crown of the hill. It is densely packed with inns, restaurants and souvenir shops, much as it would have been a thousand years ago when the abbey was the focus of an enormously popular pilgrimage and the narrow street bustled with pilgrims.

The abbey became an important spiritual and intellectual hub, and vied with other great pilgrimage centres such as Rome and Santiago de Compostela. The complex was fortified in 1256, and managed to withstand numerous attacks and sieges, particularly during the Hundred Years War (1337–1453), when Mont-St-Michel was the only part of northwestern France to remain constantly in French hands. It was said that the islet was protected by St Michael. Pilgrims continued to pour in, although many were lost in the unpredictable mists and treacherous sandbanks that blighted the approach to the islet. From the 14th century, inns, taverns and shops selling amulets and curios sprang up along the island's single road.

During the 18th century, the abbey fell into decline and the community diminished considerably: the monks left in 1790. During the French Revolution, the abbey became a prison for political prisoners, and remained so until 1863. It was declared an historic monument by the French government in 1873, and a comprehensive restoration programme was begun the following year. The slender spire with its statue of St Michael was added, and a 900-metre (2,953-ft) causeway was built to join the mont with the mainland. This manmade causeway led to the silting of the bay and extreme tides – still the highest in Europe. The causeway is currently being dismantled and replaced with a ford and pedestrian bridge that will restore the island's character by ensuring that it is cut off by water for several hours a day. Since 1966, a small community of monks has once again inhabited the abbey.

The abbey that crowns the islet displays some highly advanced engineering for the period. The most remarkable section is La Merveille, the three-storey Gothic addition clinging to the island's northern flank.

LOIRE VALLEY

Latitude 47°23'N **Longitude** 0°42'E

Location Central France

Built Most châteaux date from the 16th century

Approximate area 22,000 square kilometres (8,500 sq miles)

Official language French

Currency The euro

The great River Loire flows serenely through a broad, verdant valley full of orchards and vineyards south of Paris. The banks are dotted with dozens of glorious châteaux, which appear like visions from a fairytale. Once, there were more than 300 châteaux here, but fewer than 50 have survived. Most were built in the 16th century, some from the remains of older fortified dwellings. Their extragant beauty, architectural audacity and magnificent gardens stand testament to the ideals of the Renaissance, when the glittering French court was the envy of all Europe.

The Château de Chambord is the most spectacular of the Loire palaces, emerging like a mirage from the middle of a dense forest. It was commissioned as a splendid hunting lodge by François I (1494–1517), the first Renaissance king of France, who was celebrated for his humanist ideals and patronage of the arts. It was built in the style of the early Italian Renaissance castles of northern Italy, and some have suggested that Leonardo da Vinci, who had been enticed to the French court by François, was reponsible for its design. The château boasts 426 rooms and 77 staircases, of which the most extraordinary is the double-helix marble staircase, which forms the castle's centrepiece.

For all its splendour, the Château de Chambord is just one of the opulent building projects initiated by François I.

TRAVELLER'S TIPS

Best time to go: Avoid mid-July to late August, when the area can become very crowded with foreign tourists as well as French holiday-makers.

Look out for: The region's wines, such as whites from the Chenin blanc, Sauvignon blanc and Melon de Bourgogne grapes.

Dos and don'ts: The Loire Valley is a large region, so for ease of visiting base yourself in more than one of its picturesque towns, such as Tours and Orléans.

Chambord is the largest château in the Loire Valley, and one of its most magnficent. But, for all its extravagance and splendour, François I spent only a few weeks here – and never finally completed it.

Of all the surviving Loire châteaux, the castle at Chenonceau is perhaps the most romantic, elegantly spanning the water and supported by a series of graceful arches. Thomas Bohier, chamberlain to Charles VIII of France, ordered the construction of the new palace in 1515, and he and his wife Catherine regularly hosted royal guests there.

His childhood home, the Château d'Amboise, was an eighth-century AD fortress substantially remodelled into a grand Gothic palace by Charles VIII (1470–98). During the early years of François' reign, the château reached the pinnacle of its splendour. Leonardo da Vinci was invited to reside in the Clos Lucé, a grand mansion located 500 metres (1,600 ft) from the château, to which it was linked by an underground passage. According to popular myth, the artist died in the arms of the French king. Later owners, unable to pay for the upkeep of such an enormous complex, were forced to demolish whole wings. But, even diminished, it remains a breathtaking sight, gazing out from a rocky spur across the Loire.

The story of the Château d'Amboise parallels that of the Château de Blois, which dates back to the ninth century AD but was remodelled by Charles d'Orléans, and then by his son, Louis XII (1462–1515). François I added a Renaissance wing endowed with a magnificent spiral staircase. Mary Stuart, Queen of Scotland, grew up here, and her scheming mother-in-law, Catherine of Medici, preferred it above all other royal residences. A cabinet which reputedly contained the poisons with which she eliminated her rivals remains here.

The charming Renaissance Château d'Azay-le-Rideau, built between 1515 and1527, is another jewel on the Loire. Built in a fusion of Italianate and French styles, it was commissioned by Gilles Berthelot, treasurer to François I, who confiscated it after Berthelot was accused of embezzlement. The château, long forgotten and neglected, became popular with Romantic writers and artists at the end of the 19th century.

The château at Chenonceau belonged to Diane de Poitiers, mistress to Henri II, who adored her waterside home. She commissioned the graceful arched bridge which now connects it to the opposite bank of the river.

PARIS

Latitude 48°51'N **Longitude** 2°21'E

Location Northern France

Population 2,203,000

Approximate area 87 square kilometres
(34 sq miles)

Official language French

Currency The euro

Nowhere evokes romance quite like Paris. La Ville Lumière (The City of Lights) has been eulogized by poets, painters, novelists and film-makers: the slow-moving Seine, with its *bouquinistes* (secondhand booksellers) and cobbled quays, is perfect for romantic strolls; the pavement cafés and chic bistrots are made for dining à deux; and its gilded palaces and grand boulevards, overlooked by the omnipresent silhouette of the Eiffel Tower, provide a gloriously cinematic backdrop.

Paris began 2,000 years ago as a small Roman settlement on the Ile de la Cité, one of two natural islands in the middle of the Seine. The city had cemented its position as the greatest in Europe and a renowned centre of learning by the 12th century, when the great cathedral of Notre Dame was begun. Its enormous façade, pierced by a rose window and studded with statues of the saints, still gazes out majestically over the river below. The cathedral was badly damaged during the French Revolution and was almost in ruins when Victor Hugo made it famous in his 1831 novel *Notre Dame de Paris*. It was vigorously restored in the latter half of the 19th century, and today visitors can climb the towers and stroll among the Gothic gargoyles which leer from the upper galleries.

At about the same time that Notre Dame was rising on the Ile de la Cité, a massive fortress was being constructed on the right bank of the Seine. This would develop into a lavish palace complex, modified by several French monarchs until it became the preferred residence of François I (1494–1547), friend to Leonardo da Vinci and patron of the arts. He acquired a superb art collection which would later provide the kernel for the

The graceful Basilique du Sacré-Cœur (Basilica of the Sacred Heart) crowns the hilltop of Montmartre, and offers extraordinary views across the city. Montmartre, once a bohemian *quartier* infamous for absinthe and the cancan, is still a lively entertainment district.

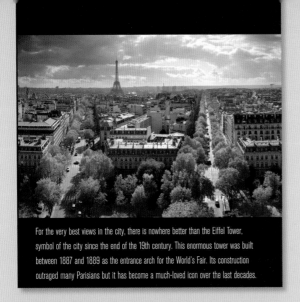

For the very best views in the city, there is nowhere better than the Eiffel Tower, symbol of the city since the end of the 19th century. This enormous tower was built between 1887 and 1889 as the entrance arch for the World's Fair. Its construction outraged many Parisians but it has become a much-loved icon over the last decades.

Louvre Museum, one of the greatest museums in the world, with a staggering array of masterpieces, presided over by Leonardo da Vinci's inscrutable *Mona Lisa* (c. 1503–06).

In the 19th century, Paris was utterly transformed by Baron Haussman: the medieval maze of old Paris was razed and replaced by broad boulevards lined with stately apartment blocks, overlooking public parks and expansive squares. Some pockets of the higgledy-piggledy old city survive, most deliciously in the Ancien Cloître, a tangle of little streets in the shadow of Notre Dame, and across the river in the Marais, now one of the most chic neighbourhoods in central Paris. Many of the aristocratic mansions ('*hôtels*') that survive here are now museums, such as the celebrated Picasso Museum.

The Plâce de la Bastille, a short stroll east, is where the *ancien régime* met its end in 1789, when a mob stormed the infamous Bastille fortress. A symbol of royal despotism, it was quickly demolished – triggering the French Revolution. Now, the square is overlooked by the glassy Opéra Bastille, inaugurated on the 200th anniversary of the storming of the Bastille.

Paris' historic night-time hotspot was the bohemian neighbourhood of Montmartre, spilling down a steep hill in the north of the city. At the turn of the 20th century, it was the art centre of the world, a magnet for painters, writers and intellectuals, who gathered in taverns and music halls. Now scrubbed up, Montmartre has lost its old raffish charm, but its steep cobbled streets, flower-filled balconies and magnificent views make it worth the trip.

The Ile de la Cité, a small island in the Seine, is where Paris began. It is still crowned by the soaring spire of the 12th-century cathedral of Notre Dame, one of the finest French Gothic buildings in the world.

BRUGES

Bruges, sometimes called the 'Venice of the North', has none of the flamboyance of its southern sister, but shares its watery soul. Like Venice, Bruges made its fortune with maritime trade during the Middle Ages, and its medieval streets are stitched together with a network of canals. Historically the most important trading city of Flanders, it is now the capital of Belgium's Flemish region.

Bruges (Brugge in Flemish) received its city charter in 1128 and became an important textile centre. Between the 13th and 15th centuries, Bruges experienced a glorious Golden Age,

Latitude 51°13'N **Longitude** 3°14'E

Location West Flanders, Belgium

Population 117,000

Approximate area 138 square kilometres (53 sq miles)

Official languages Flemish, French and German, but Bruges lies in Belgium's Flemish region

Currency The euro

TRAVELLER'S **TIPS**

Best time to go: Bruges is a popular year-round destination. Visit in winter to see the medieval buildings dusted with snow, or in spring to enjoy the blossom.

Look out for: The De Halve Maan brewery is the only one to survive in central Bruges. It has won numerous awards for its Brugse Zot beer.

Dos and don'ts: Do attempt to speak Flemish, but don't be surprised if locals prefer to speak English rather than French.

when merchants from across Europe and beyond converged on the city, trading in everything from Levantine spices to English wool. Most of the beautifully preserved medieval city that enchants modern visitors dates from this period, an ensemble of impressive mansions, churches and civic buildings.

The heart of the city is the Grote Markt (Big Market Square), flanked by gabled townhouses and still the site of a weekly market. It is overlooked by the Belfort, a mighty belltower begun in the 13th century, which has become the city's symbol. The nearby square of the Burg is even grander,

The canals and rivers made the city's fortune during its medieval Golden Age, when huge ships would traverse these waters.

dominated by the Gothic façade of Belgium's oldest city hall, and the 12th-century Heilig Bloedbasiliek (Basilica of the Holy Blood). This contains a precious relic: a vial of blood supposedly wiped from the body of Christ by Joseph of Arimathea.

Dynastic alliances had brought Flanders under the control of the Duchy of Burgundy by the end of the 14th century.

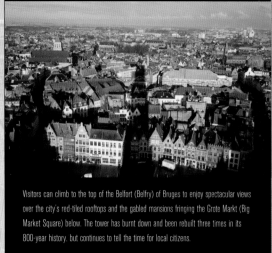

Visitors can climb to the top of the Belfort (Belfry) of Bruges to enjoy spectacular views over the city's red-tiled rooftops and the gabled mansions fringing the Grote Markt (Big Market Square) below. The tower has burnt down and been rebuilt three times in its 800-year history, but continues to tell the time for local citizens.

The Burgundian court established at Bruges became famous for its patronage of the arts, particularly painting. Jan van Eyck (c. 1395–1441) was the most celebrated of the painters nurtured in Bruges, and his work, along with that of other so-called Flemish Primitives, is among the highlights of the fascinating Groeningemuseum. Other outstanding museums in Bruges include the Memling collection, displayed in a 12th-century hospital, with just six exquisite works from the 15th-century artist.

The Begijnhof occupies the prettiest and most tranquil corner of Bruges, surrounded by a web of tranquil canals. It is a pretty complex of low, white-painted gabled houses connected by cobbled passages, and was first constructed in the 13th century for the Beguines, members of a lay religious order. Now occupied by Benedictine nuns, it remains a hushed and contemplative spot. The watery expanse of the nearby Minnewater – where ships from around the world once moored at the bustling docks – is now silent and dreamy, a wonderful spot for quiet strolls. There are fine views back to the city spires from its pretty bridges.

Paradoxically, Bruges' decline as a shipping power from the end of the 16th century would later make its fortune. For more than 200 years, almost nothing changed in this quiet backwater, which was eclipsed by Antwerp as the preeminent Flemish port. With its medieval heritage virtually untouched, by the end of the 19th century the little city was discovered by a burgeoning tourist industry. The cobbled streets are now lined with souvenir shops (chocolates and lace are popular buys), and the gabled mansions contain fine restaurants.

Bruges's bustling Grote Markt is the heart of this thriving city. A popular attraction for tourists, its gabled, Gothic-style buildings feature a wide range of restaurants, brasseries, cafés and hotels.

NEUSCHWANSTEIN

Latitude 47°33'N **Longitude** 10°44'E

Location Bavaria, Germany

Built 1869

Materials Steel, brick, limestone

Official language German

Currency The euro

Neuschwanstein is the very embodiment of a castle from the pages of a story-book, its slender spires emerging from thick forest high in the Bavarian mountains. It was built for the eccentric King Ludwig II of Bavaria (1845–86), who commissioned numerous fantasy castles during his reign. The castle was the inspiration for Sleeping Beauty's castle in Disneyland, and played a central role in the classic children's film *Chitty Chitty Bang Bang*. Ludwig was eventually deposed by conspirators within his own government, who had him declared insane by doctors who had never even met him.

By the time of Ludwig II's mysterious death (he was found drowned in the lake by Neuschwanstein), the castle was almost finished. However, its lavish construction had so drained the king's finances that it was almost immediately opened to visitors in order to pay for its completion.

Ludwig was an ardent admirer of the composer Richard Wagner, who completed several great works, including *Tristan und Isolde* (1865), under the king's patronage. Unfortunately, Ludwig was asked to exile Wagner from Munich, after the composer's scandalous love affairs outraged the conservative Bavarian court. But Wagner would continue to deeply influence the young king, who conceived of a fantasy castle which would be 'a worthy temple for the divine friend who has brought salvation and true blessing to the world'. This castle was Schloss Neuschwanstein, begun in 1869.

Neuschwanstein was conceived as an ideal residence for the Swan Knight Lohengrin, a medieval knight of German Athurian legend and the hero of Wagner's eponymous opera. Its walls were richly decorated with depictions of medieval sagas (many of which were subjects in Wagner's compositions). Ludwig even commissioned a Singer's Hall, a special theatre where Wagner could work and stage his operas. For all its medieval romance, however, the castle made use of the modern technology available, from electricity to plumbing and even an early telephone system.

Schloss Neuschwanstein emerges like a mirage from the clouds swathing the Bavarian mountains.

TRAVELLER'S **TIPS**

Best time to go: Spring and autumn are the best times to visit: the summer months are very crowded, and it gets dark early in winter.

Look out for: The Marienbrücke pedestrian bridge crosses a deep gorge with a waterfall, and offers a superb panorama of the castle.

Dos and don'ts: Don't take pictures inside: photography is forbidden. Instead, postcards and books can be bought in the souvenir shop.

HAMMERFEST

Latitude 70°39'N **Longitude** 23°41'E

Location Finnmark, Norway

Population 9,200

Approximate area 849 square kilometres (328 sq miles) including all its rural districts

Official language Norwegian

Currency The krone

Hammerfest is the northernmost city in the world, a neat little conurbation tucked around a wide harbour on the western end of the remote island of Kvaløya. At this latitude, the Sun does not set for two and a half months during the summer, while an eerie twilight reigns for much of the winter, when the Sun never rises above the horizon. But Hammerfest is famous above all for being one of the best places to see the Northern Lights, a spectacular natural phenomenon that occurs near the North Pole.

These strange, swirling lights, with their shifting forms and multicoloured hues, fill the sky nightly during the dark winter months in Hammerfest. They might be seen any time from October to March, but they are most common between mid-November and mid-January. The Northern Lights are also known as *aurora borealis*, meaning 'northern dawn', and were named for the Roman goddess who races across the morning sky in her chariot by a French academic, Pierre Gassend, in the 17th century.

The phenomenon occurs because of the interaction between particles from the Sun (known as 'solar wind') and the Earth's atmosphere: as the charged solar particles collide with the Earth's air, they emit energy in the form of light. This happens only near the North and South Poles because these are not protected by the Earth's magnetic field. The different gases present in the atmosphere provide the kaleidoscope of colours, although greenish and red shades usually predominate. Science may explain the phenomenon, but most of the thousands of visitors who come to watch the lights dance and twirl in the night sky are simply struck by their otherworldly magic.

One of the oldest settlements above the Arctic Circle, Hammerfest has a history dating back 5,000 years. The little city is ringed with hills, offering spectacular views over the lakes and coastline. The North Cape, a steep headland on a nearby island (reached by a daily boat), rewards visitors with glimpses of eagles, orcas and seals.

TRAVELLER'S **TIPS**

Best time to go: The Northern Lights occur between October and March, but they are most commonly seen between mid-November and mid-January.

Look out for: Huge herds of reindeer migrate from their winter pastures and descend on Hammerfest during the summer months.

Dos and don'ts: Do pick up a copy of Bill Bryson's *Neither Here nor There*, which features Hammerfest and describes the Northern Lights.

ROME

Latitude 41°54'N **Longitude** 12°13'E

Location Central Italy

Population 2,700,000

Approximate area 1,285 square kilometres (496 sq miles)

Official language Italian

Currency The euro

For a thousand years, Rome was the most powerful city on Earth. The 'Eternal City' was capital of the vast Roman empire, which once encompassed most of Europe and the Mediterranean. The early Romans built as though their civilization would last forever, and their astounding monuments are still breathtaking. The ancient city was later shaped by the splendour of the Renaissance and the opulence of Baroque to become the theatrical beauty immortalized in Fellini's *La Dolce Vita* (1960).

The Colosseum, a vast, elliptical amphitheatre, still dominates Rome's historic centre after two millennia. The largest amphitheatre ever built in the empire, it could accommodate a staggering 50,000 spectators. In AD 80, the Emperor Titus hosted a huge inaugural gala during which 9,000 beasts were massacred, and it is thought as many as half a million people lost their lives in gladiatorial combat. The exterior of the amphitheatre has survived extraordinarily intact, and has become an icon of the city. The Forum – the social, political, religious and commercial centre of ancient Rome – has fared less well, but the sheer scale of its romantically ruined temples and gates, arches and sacred ways, still evoke its former grandeur.

The Ponte'Sant Angelo, formerly the Pons Aelius, has spanned the Tiber since the second century AD, but has been remodelled several times.

Very little remains of the ancient Forum, which was once the very heart and soul of the Roman empire and contained all its most important commercial, political and religious institutions. Evocative fragments of temples, columns and gateways are all that survive of this once-vibrant heart of the Roman empire.

Rome's Colosseum was the largest ever built in the Roman empire, a massive auditorium dedicated to gladiatorial combat, animal hunts and other bloody spectacles. The ruined interior is no longer used for entertainment, but several major concerts have taken place with the iconic Colosseum forming a theatrical backdrop.

The best preserved of all Rome's ancient monuments is the Pantheon, a temple erected in the first century AD and dedicated to all the city's gods. It was converted into a Christian church in AD 609, and, although the interior has been superficially remodelled in subsequent years, the ancient temple has survived virtually intact. Its domed roof is still the largest unreinforced concrete dome in the world. The Pantheon stands on the fringes of the atmospheric neighbourhood usually known simply as Old Rome. A maze of narrow streets, it also contains some of the city's most beautiful squares. Perhaps finest among them is the Piazza Navona, a glorious Baroque showpiece laid out in the 17th century. The famous Piazza di Spagna is overlooked by the grand swoop of the Spanish Steps, a lavish Baroque double staircase. Even more famous is the Fontana di Trevi, in which an electrifying Anita Ekberg cavorted in Fellini's *La Dolce Vita*.

Rome is also the spiritual headquarters of the Roman Catholic Church, and Vatican City occupies a hilltop on the west bank of the Tiber River. It is the smallest country in the world at just 0.4 square kilometres (0.2 sq miles), yet it contains the world's largest church, museum and square. The Piazza di San Pietro is dominated by the Basilica di San Pietro (Basilica of Saint Peter), built between the 16th and 18th centuries and filled with artistic treasures, including Michelangelo's moving *Pietà* (1499). The Vatican apartments contain several outstanding museums, but the most famous attraction is Michelangelo's painted ceiling for the Sistine Chapel. These biblical scenes, painted between 1508 and 1512, are among the most powerful images in the Western canon. *The Last Judgement*, painted more than two decades after the ceiling, is an infinitely darker, but no less stirring, work.

The Basilica di San Pietro is crowned with an enormous dome designed by Michelangelo, richly decorated with mosaic and stucco.

VENICE

Latitude 45°25'N **Longitude** 12°19'E

Location Veneto, Italy

Population 60,000

Approximate area 415 square kilometres (160 sq miles)

Official language Italian, with Venet occasionally spoken

Currency The euro

According to myth, Venice – like Venus, the goddess of love – was born miraculously from the sea. It grew from a collection of diminutive islands scattered across a marshy lagoon to become the most powerful city-state in Italy. The Most Serene Republic of Venice, 'La Serenissima', endured for a thousand years, and its luminous beauty has been celebrated by artists from Titian to Tintoretto. Modern Venice remains an enchanting time-capsule, and its ancient *palazzi* and churches, reflected in the dappled waters of the narrow canals, still bear witness to its glorious past.

The Grand Canal is lined with Renaissance mansions. Slim, wooden boats bob next to ancient piers, and gondolas and river taxis ply the waters.

Venice's strategic location on the Adriatic Sea, at the very cusp of east and west trading routes, would make its fortune: by the end of the 13th century, it was the richest city in Europe. Its merchants vied with each other to commission the most splendid *palazzi*, and fill them with works of art. Although Western art and architectural traditions predominated, the subtle influence of the East is also evident in delicately sculpted horseshoe arches and the burnished gleam of Byzantine mosaics. The most celebrated of these grand Gothic mansions is the Palazzo Ducale, constructed for the Doge between 1309 and 1424, which gazes out across the Piazza San Marco. This is the city's dazzling main square, named for the

patron saint of Venice, the evangelist St Mark, whose symbol, the winged lion, is found throughout the city (including above the main portal of the Palazzo Ducale). His importance to Venice dates back to the ninth century AD, when the saint's relics were stolen from Alexandria by Venetian merchants. They are kept in the Basilica di San Marco, perhaps the most famous Byzantine church in the world, which was consecrated in 1094 and adjoins the Palazzo Ducale. Richly gilded mosaics depicting scenes from the saint's life adorn the main façade and encrust the cavernous interior with shimmering colour. The effect is startling, and it is immediately evident why the basilica has long been nicknamed the Chiesa d'Oro (Golden

TRAVELLER'S **TIPS**

Best time to go: The tourist season peaks in July and August. Ideal months to visit are May, June and September, but to avoid the crowds, visit in winter.

Look out for: Murano glass. The colourful glass from the Venetian island of Murano has been made for centuries.

Dos and don'ts: Do spend the night: many of Venice's visitors are day-trippers, but the city is magical at night. Do use the fast river buses

The city has been battling the Adriatic Sea throughout its existence, but the flooding (*aqua alta*, or 'high water') has become acute, occurring as often as once or twice a week in recent years. The Piazza di San Marco is regularly underwater. A flood barrier is being erected in the lagoon, but opinion is divided about its long-term effectiveness.

Church). The bronze horses that project from the terrace above the entrance were looted from Constantinople by the Doge in the mid-13th century. These are copies of the forth century BC originals, which are kept in the Basilica Museum.

Modern Venice comprises 118 islands linked by 177 canals. The Grand Canal remains the most important of Venice's waterways and still exudes an ineffable romance despite the constant traffic of *vaporettos* (water buses) and water taxis. The most lavish of the city's mansions overlook the waterway, which has been the city's grandest address since the Middle Ages. Among the most beautiful edifices is the 15th-century Ca' d'Oro (now an art gallery), with a creamy, intricately sculpted façade; the Renaissance-style Palazzo Vendramin (now the Casino); and the Venetian Gothic Palazzo Dario. The latter occasionally hosts art exhibitions for the Peggy Guggenheim Collection, which has its main seat in the 18th-century Palazzo Venier dei Leoni, which also overlooks the canal.

The Gallerie dell'Accademia, the city's most prestigious art museum, is located in a resplendent neoclassical building near the Accademia bridge. The museum contains a superb collection of Venetian paintings which, with portraits of notable historical figures and unchanged cityscapes, offer a fascinating glimpse into the past. One of the city's newest museums occupies the Palazzo Grimani, a sumptuous mansion built in the 16th century for Antonio Grimani, who rose from humble origins to become Venice's Doge. The palace was remodelled in the 16th century, and is replete with frescoes, inlaid marble floors and gorgeous artworks.

Piazza San Marco is the heart of Venice, overlooked by the most important buildings in the city: the Basilica di San Marco and the extravagant Palazzo Ducale with its intricately sculpted Renaissance façade.

METÉORA

Latitude 39°42'N **Longitude** 21°37'E

Location Near Kalambaka, Thessaly, Central Greece

Built 11th–15th centuries

Materials Stone

Official language Greek

Currency The euro

The name Metéora comes from a Greek word meaning 'suspended in the sky', and this collection of medieval Orthodox monasteries, perched impossibly on jagged pinnacles, seems to be just that. The sandstone rocks, sculpted by the elements into a forest of natural towers, erupt dramatically from the northwestern corner of the Plain of Thessaly in central Greece. This beautiful landscape has been a religious retreat since the 11th century.

Those early hermits inhabited the natural caves scored into one of the thousand or so sandstone pinnacles. In 1336, the first monastery complex was consecrated atop one of the loftiest peaks, its congregation laboriously hauled by rope up the steep slopes. This was the Great Meteoron, also known as the Monastery of the Transfiguration of Christ. It is the oldest, and still the highest and grandest, of the surviving monasteries, and has been converted into a fascinating museum. A century later, there were more than 20 monasteries in the Metéora region – but they flourished only briefly, before slipping into decline.

Only six of the monasteries remain, with much reduced religious communities. However, they have gained a new lease of life in recent decades and function largely as museums for the deluge of visitors who arrive daily, slogging up steep paths carved into the rock in the 1920s.

TRAVELLER'S TIPS

Best time to go: Spring (April to June) is the ideal time to visit. From September to November temperatures are mild (July and August are very hot).

Look out for: Hikers, climbers and bird-watchers. This region offers numerous opportunities for outdoor activities, and is a mecca for rock-climbers.

Dos and don'ts: Do be prepared for cooler weather high up. Dress appropriately if you want to enter the monasteries: dress codes are strictly enforced.

The dream-like pinnacles of Metéora have been a sacred retreat for more than a thousand years. Two dozen monasteries once flourished here, of which only six survive, but the area's enduring tranquility and natural beauty continue to invite contemplation.

ST PETERSBURG

Latitude 59°57'N **Longitude** 30°19'E

Location Northwestern Federal District, Russia

Population 4,600,000

Approximate area 1,439 square kilometres
(556 sq miles)

Official language Russian (most street signs are in
the Cyrillic alphabet)

Currency The rouble

St Petersburg was conceived by Peter the Great (1672–1725)
as a glittering, modern capital for the emerging Russian
empire. It remained capital for 200 years, and the sumptuous
historic centre, replete with gilded palaces, still evokes the
grandeur of Tsarist Russia. Shattered first by the aftermath of
the Russian Revolution in 1917, St Petersburg (rechristened
Leningrad by the Soviets) was devastated by the Siege of
Leningrad between 1941 and 1943. It was one of the longest,
bloodiest and most destructive sieges in modern history: more
than one and a half million people died, many of starvation,
and another one and a half million were displaced. The
reconstruction of the city took several decades, but St
Petersburg is now listed by UNESCO as a World Heritage Site
and is renowned as the most cultured city in Russia.

TRAVELLER'S TIPS

Best time to go: The long nights of summer, when the Sun barely sets, make
it the ideal time to visit St Petersburg.

Look out for: At the end of the summer White Nights Festival of performing arts,
a beautiful historic ship with billowing red sails glides down the Neva River.

Dos and don'ts: Do dress appropriately – average temperatures in January are
-13 to -8°C (9–18°F). Do use the metro to admire the Art Deco stations.

When Peter the Great chose this spot for his new city, it was remote and swampy, and very few of his courtly companions shared his vision. But the Tsar ordered his nobles to build new mansions here, and compelled them to remain in the capital for at least six months a year. This command was unpopular, but it bequeathed the slew of beautiful Baroque palaces with which the city is endowed. Peter the Great wanted his new capital to emulate the great cities of the west, and rejected homegrown Russian architecture in favour of the Baroque and Neoclassical styles then prevalent in western capitals.

St Isaac's Cathedral, with its dome hovering above the frozen Neva River, was the largest church in Russia when it was built (1818–58).

In a departure from the Baroque and Neoclassical styles which predominate in St Petersburg, the Church of Our Saviour on Spilled Blood is a romantic, neo-medieval structure topped with golden onion domes and glimmering, Byzantine-style mosaics. It was built in memory of Alexander II, who was fatally stabbed on this spot in 1881.

The earliest building in St Petersburg is the Peter and Paul Fortress, a citadel erected to defend the nascent city from the Swedish army during the Great Northern War (1700–21). It was later rebuilt in lavish Baroque fashion, and a number of important buildings were commissioned within the complex. The finest of these is the Peter and Paul Cathedral, begun in 1712 to designs by Domenico Trezzini, court architect to Peter the Great. The splendid Baroque church is a pantheon of Russian monarchs, and the remains of all but two tsars from Peter the Great until Nicholas II (1868–1918) are buried here. The golden spire is topped with an image of the

Angel with a Cross, which has become a much-loved symbol of the city. Another of the famous buildings found within the fortress is the Mint, established by Peter the Great (although now hidden behind high security fences), which still mints Russian coins.

The most beautiful and celebrated of the city's palaces is the Winter Palace, built between 1754 and 1762 for the Empress Elizabeth Petrovna, daughter of Peter the Great. It became the official residence of the imperial family until they were ousted in 1917. It is a lavish, Rococo confection and overlooks the

splendid Palace Square on one side and the Neva River on the other. The Winter Palace is now the centrepiece of a series of imperial residences which include the Small Hermitage and the Great Hermitage, which have been collectively converted into the world-famous Hermitage Museum. Catherine the Great (1729–96) founded the museum in 1764, when she purchased a collection of 255 paintings from Berlin. In the early years, it was a private museum, but it opened its doors to the public in 1852. Now, the Hermitage boasts almost three million objects, which form one of the most prestigious collections in the world.

The Hermitage Museum is the world's largest art museum. It occupies the magnificent Winter Palace, former residence of the Russian tsars.

The Alexander Column dominates Palace Square, the vast public square in central St Petersburg. The column was built in the early 19th century to commemorate the Russian victory over Napoleon's armies, and is named for Alexander I. It is topped by a bronze angel, which is said to resemble the emperor. At 47 metres (154 ft), the column is the tallest of its kind in the world.

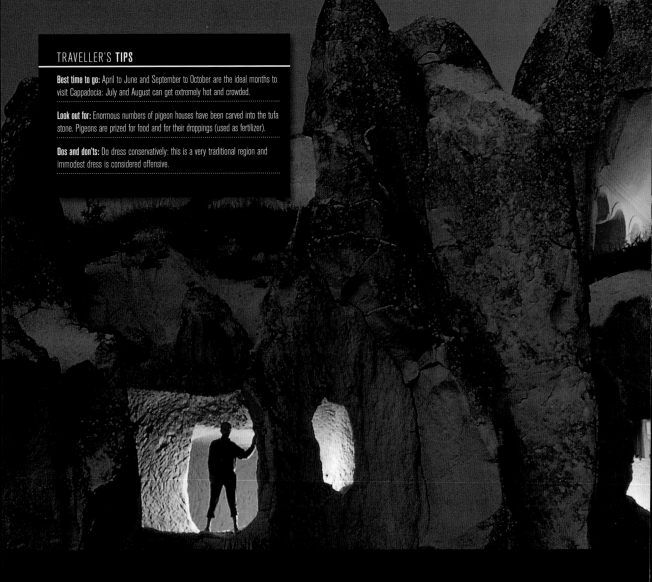

TRAVELLER'S **TIPS**

Best time to go: April to June and September to October are the ideal months to visit Cappadocia: July and August can get extremely hot and crowded.

Look out for: Enormous numbers of pigeon houses have been carved into the tufa stone. Pigeons are prized for food and for their droppings (used as fertilizer).

Dos and don'ts: Do dress conservatively: this is a very traditional region and immodest dress is considered offensive.

CAPPADOCIA

Latitude 38°37'N **Longitude** 34°43'E

Location Central Anatolia, Turkey

Approximate area 70,000 square kilometres (27,000 sq miles)

Approximate dimensions 400 kilometres (250 miles) east-west. 200 kilometres (120 miles) north-south

Official language Turkish

Currency Turkish lira

Cappadocia is an ancient region of central Turkey that has long been famed for its surreal landscape of rocky pinnacles fancifully described as 'fairy chimneys'. Most of these are centred on the town of Göreme, now the focus of a national park that has been designated a UNESCO World Heritage Site. The region's unique natural wonders are equalled by the houses, churches and monasteries, and even entire underground cities, that have been carved into the soft rock over the millennia.

The region is riddled with as many as 300 underground cities, excavated as early as Hittite times (c. 1750–1180 BC). The Hittites

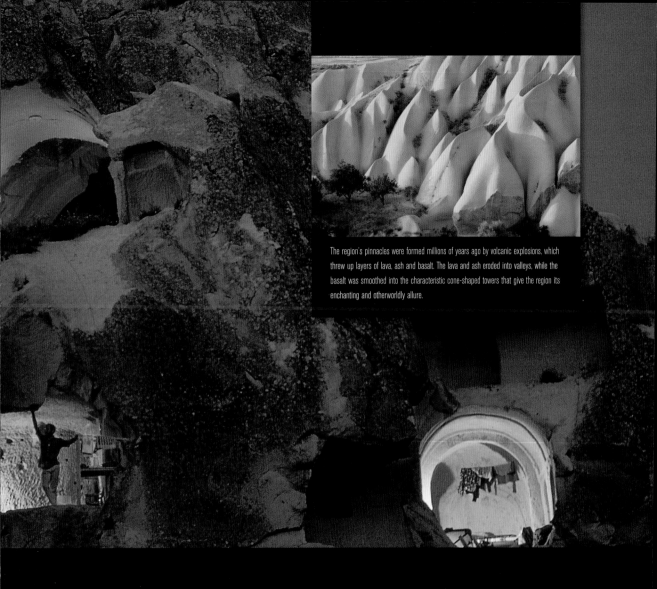

The region's pinnacles were formed millions of years ago by volcanic explosions, which threw up layers of lava, ash and basalt. The lava and ash eroded into valleys, while the basalt was smoothed into the characteristic cone-shaped towers that give the region its enchanting and otherworldly allure.

were evading marauding armies, and they were followed some centuries later by the early Christians, attempting to escape persecution. Derinkuyu is the deepest of the discovered cities, with at least 11 floors extending 85 metres (280 ft) underground. Despite their size, it seems unlikely that the cities were ever intended as permanent settlements, but were built to provide a safe retreat in the event of attack.

Cappadocia began to attract small communities of anchorites (hermits) from around the fourth century AD. Many of them congregated around Göreme, which rapidly developed into a

Many of Göreme's 'fairy chimneys' have been carved into dwellings and are still used as homes, storehouses and even hotels.

major Christian monastic centre. The largest and most beautiful monastic complex to survive is now preserved as the Göreme Open Air Museum, which contains more than 30 churches, refectories and other religious buildings carved into the rock between the 10th and 12th centuries. The buildings are decorated with dazzling Byzantine frescoes, dating from AD 900 to 1200 and still wonderfully vivid.

CAPPADOCIA

PETRA

Petra
◇
JORDAN

Latitude 30°19'N **Longitude** 35°28'E

Location Arabah, Jordan

Built c. 3rd century BC–7th century AD

Materials Sandstone

Official language Arabic, with English widely used among officials and businesspeople

Currency Jordanian dinar

The ancient city of Petra was carved into the sandstone walls of desert canyons more than 2,000 years ago. The Nabateans, a formerly nomadic people, arrived in the third century BC, and transformed what had been a remote desert settlement into a wealthy metropolis. The extensive remains of this glorious city had lain virtually untouched for several centuries when the Swiss explorer Johann Ludwig Burckhardt came upon them in 1812. Now the site, recently declared one of the New Seven Wonders of the World, attracts half a million people a year.

Petra owed its wealth to its strategic location at the crux of several important trading routes that linked the Red Sea and the Mediterranean. Huge caravans regularly crossed the mountains with valuable cargoes bound for Rome. The Nabateans provided the travellers with safe passage through the canyons, as well as food and shelter. Petra grew rapidly: at its peak, it may have been home to as many as 20,000 people. The constant flow of travellers imbued Petra with influences from several civilizations, including the Egyptian, Mesopotamian, Greek and Roman, all of which are evident in the architecture.

The architecture of El Khazneh (The Treasury), built between 100 BC and AD 200, was influenced by the classical Greek style.

TRAVELLER'S TIPS

Best time to go: Spring and early autumn, when the light is at its best and the weather is temperate. Winter can be extremely cold and wet.

Look out for: The small, on-site museum, which contains pottery, fragments of carved stone and all kinds of interesting artefacts.

Dos and don'ts: Don't leave rubbish or cigarette butts. Do consider the detrimental environmental impact of some tourist services, such as helicopter rides.

Modern visitors approach Petra through the Siq, a narrow ravine enclosed by towering walls of red stone. It was once the ceremonial entrance to the religious area of the city, and its walls are pocked with small niches that would once have contained votive images, as well as the vestiges of a carving of a camel and camel drivers.

By the time the Romans took the city over in AD 104, Petra was flourishing. It continued to prosper for at least another century, but the opening up of new trade routes began to erode Petra's influence. In AD 363, it was badly damaged by an earthquake, which hastened its decline. It appears that Petra's function became increasingly religious, and it was abandoned some time during the early seventh century.

As visitors approach Petra through the narrow ravine known as the Siq, there are tantalising glimpses of El Khazneh (The Treasury). According to locals, it got its name from the Bedouin, who believed that the urns carved into the façade contained treasure. In fact, El Khazneh is a lavish tomb, carved directly into the cliff face. The interior, like all the tombs in Petra, is small and plain. It is best seen in the morning, when sunlight sparkles on the rock face. The canyon opens out into a wider space that was the teeming heart of the city. Nearby is the Theatre, built in the first century AD, and later enlarged by the Romans. Along the Street of the Façades, several tombs are etched into the rock face, including the famous Urn Tomb. One of the most heart-stopping views of the site is found at the High Place of Sacrifice. Sacrifices may have been made to the gods from an 'altar' on the site, but evidence is scant. From here, there are splendid views of Ed-Deir, the largest and one of the most elaborate of Petra's surviving tombs. Built in the first century BC and dedicated to Obodas I, it boasts a magnificent façade with tiers of carved columns.

Ed-Deir (The Monastery) was dedicated to Obodas I, a deified Nabatean king who ruled during the first century BC. Ed-Deir is beautifully carved and so huge that even the doorway is several storeys tall.

ASWAN
TO LUXOR

Latitude 25°41'N **Longitude** 32°39'E

Location Southern Egypt

Transport Felucca or cruise ship

Approximate length 250 kilometres (155 miles)

Official language Arabic

Currency Egyptian pound

Aswan, the ancient gateway to Egypt, sits on the banks of the Nile, 250 kilometres (155 miles) south of the tourist mecca of Luxor. The white-sailed boats called feluccas still ply the great river, linking the two cities in time-honoured tradition. The boats glide past carefully cultivated fields, scattered with the remains of ancient temples. Feluccas have made this journey since the time of the pharaohs and provide a serene and timeless alternative to the luxurious cruise ships and motor boats that also use these waters.

At Aswan's famous bazaar, the enormous Sharia el-Suq, the babble of shoppers haggling with market traders continues much as it has for thousands of years. Down at the river, Elephant Island is one of the oldest sites in Egypt; at its southern tip is a temple to Khnum, bull-headed god of the Nile, which dates back to the 18th dynasty (1550–1292 BC). About 50 kilometres (30 miles) north of Aswan, and a slow sail by felucca, the impressive remnants of an ancient temple loom above the eastern bank of the river. This is the Temple of Kom Ombo, which dates back to the second century BC. The southern half of the temple is dedicated to the crocodile god Sobek, and the northern section to the falcon god Horus, who

TRAVELLER'S TIPS

Best time to go: It is possible to cruise the Nile year-round, but it's best to avoid July and August, which can be very hot.

Look out for: The Galabaya. The traditional Egyptian flowing robes are popular souvenirs – and very practical to beat the heat.

Dos and don'ts: Do swim only in the areas pointed out by the boat crew. Don't forget to pack a sleeping bag in winter, when nights are chilly.

The low, white-sailed feluccas have plied the waters of the Nile for thousands of years. Contemporary materials are used in their construction, but the design has remained unchanged.

was credited with healing powers. The temple was an important pilgrimage site for many centuries, but then fell into neglect. It now contains several of the mummified crocodiles found in the temple grounds.

Modern Luxor, reached after about four days' sailing from Aswan, occupies the site of ancient Thebes, the capital of Egypt during the New Kingdom (16th to 11th centuries BC). Abutting the modern city is the Temple of Luxor, founded in 1400 BC and dedicated to the god Amun, king of all the gods, as well as his consort Mut and their son Chons. Enormous statues (colossi) still preside over the temple's solemn chambers, and a road lined with sphinxes links it to the Temple of Karnak, the largest ancient religious site in the world.

Luxor is probably most famous for the Valley of the Kings, an extraordinary necropolis filled with the tombs of the great monarchs of the New Kingdom. Most dazzling of all is the gleaming tomb of the young pharaoh Tutankhamun, discovered in 1922 by the archaeologist Howard Carter, and the most complete pharaonic tomb yet discovered. The story of the young king, thought to have been only 19 when he died, captured the world's imagination, and his body, now preserved in a temperature-controlled case, remains the focus of all kinds of romantic legends – including dark stories about the 'Curse of the Pharaohs'. The nearby Valley of the Queens contains the lavishly decorated tomb of Nefertari (c.1290–1254 BC), wife of Ramesses the Great, who described her as 'the one for whom the sun shines'.

The Temple of Karnak is still awe-inspiring after more than three millennia. It was built over 1,300 years, with much of the finest work being carried out under Ramesses II, whose enormous statue was built around 1400 BC.

SKELETON COAST

NAMIBIA
◇Skeleton Coast

Latitude 19°0'S **Longitude** 12°40'E	
Location Northern Namibia	
Founded National park formed in 1973	
Approximate area Skeleton Coast National Park covers 16,000 square kilometres (6,000 sq miles)	
Official language English	
Currency Namibian dollar	

Namibian bushmen call the Skeleton Coast 'the land God made in anger'. This vast, arid and desolate stretch of Atlantic coast was named for the sea-bleached bones of whales and seals, which once littered the shore, shrouded in the mists that plague the coastline. These bones have been joined by the hulks of hundreds of shipwrecks, washed up here by treacherous currents, and inhabited by scuttling ghost crabs. It is one of the most inhospitable landscapes anywhere in the world, and yet, in the shifting colours of the desert sands, it attains a haunting beauty.

Much of the region has now been declared a national park and, although it seems impossible that any wildlife could subsist in this land, one of the world's largest seal colonies exists at Cape Fria. About 60,000 Cape fur seals waddle around the rocks, barking at scavenging jackals. Whales and dolphins can be seen off the coast. The very fortunate may even spot the endemic, but extremely rare, Heaviside dolphin. Other animals have adapted to the dry conditions, including gemsbok and springbok and even long-legged desert elephants and lions.

Among the strangest natural curiosities to be found along the Skeleton Coast are the Roaring Dunes. As people, or even vehicles, slide down the banks of the vast dunes, they emit a low rumble which gets increasingly louder until it becomes an astonishing, reverberating bellow. The pale 'castles', fanciful towers of whiteish clay, which occur in the Hoarusib Canyon, are another extraordinary natural phenomenon that should not be missed.

The Skeleton Coast is usually shrouded in a thick, treacherous mist, which has caused hundreds of boats to founder along the coastline. The skeletons of the shipwrecks have given the coast its name.

TRAVELLER'S **TIPS**

Best time to go: The Skeleton Coast is a superb year-round destination, with no real variations in the weather. For angling, November to March is best.

Look out for: The *Dunedin* is the most celebrated shipwreck on the Skeleton Coast. The ship foundered during the Second World War.

Dos and don'ts: Do wear appropriate clothing to protect you from being scoured by the sand-laden wind: long-sleeved shirts and jackets, with a hat.

VICTORIA FALLS

ZAMBIA

Victoria Falls

ZIMBABWE

Latitude 17°55'S **Longitude** 25°49'E

Location Zambia–Zimbabwe border

River Zambezi River

Approximate dimensions 1,708 metres (5,600 ft) wide, 108 metres (360 ft) high

Official language English

Currencies Zambian kwacha and Zimbabwean dollar

The vast Zambezi River begins life high in the marshy wetlands of northeastern Zambia, flowing east through Angola, then south through Namibia, Botswana, Zimbabwe and Mozambique, before emptying into the Indian Ocean. The Zambezi's flow is punctuated by several spectacular waterfalls, of which the most celebrated is the magnificent Victoria Falls, also known as Mosi-oa-Tunya, which means 'The Smoke that Thunders'. It is traditionally believed that Dr David Livingstone (1813–73), a Scottish explorer, was the first European to lay eyes on the falls, which he first saw in 1855 and renamed for his monarch.

A huge curtain of water drops from the lip of a two-kilometre-long (1.2-mile), horseshoe-shaped basalt cliff. The force and volume of the falls can be accounted for by the topography of the region: above the falls, the river moves through a wide plain, but it is increasingly channelled into a narrow basalt cleft. The water plummets over the cliff edge at the rate of around 5,000 cubic metres (16,404 cu ft) a minute during the high-water season (March–May). The water cascades between 90 and 170 metres (295 and 558 ft) into the gorge below with such force that it creates clouds of mist full of dancing rainbows that can be seen up to 50 kilometres (30 miles) away. At full moon during the high-water season, it is sometimes possible to see the heart-stopping natural phenomenon of the 'moonbow'. In low season, the volume of water can shrink by as much

TRAVELLER'S TIPS

Best time to go: The end of the rainy season (which runs from November to April) is the best time to see the falls at their most powerful.

Look out for: Full moon. When the falls are in full flow, 'moonbows' are created by the moonlight.

Dos and don'ts: Don't forget that the falls sit on an international border and you will need the appropriate visas to see them from both sides.

The Victoria Falls create a constant cloud of spray in their immediate vicinity. As a result, the rainforest that surrounds the falls is the only place in the world where it rains all day every day.

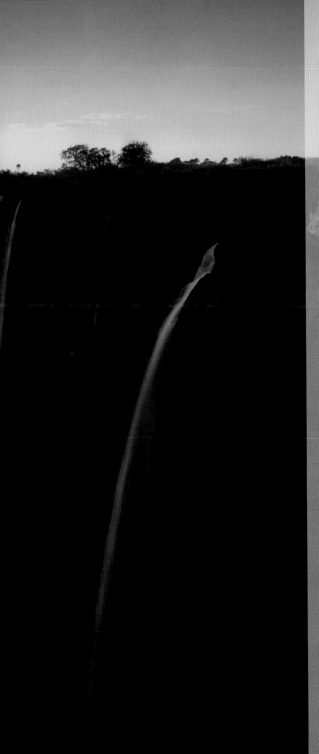

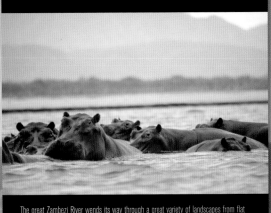

The great Zambezi River wends its way through a great variety of landscapes from flat wetlands to shadowy mangrove forests, and supports a huge variety of wildlife, including elephants, zebras, antelope and crocodiles. Hippopotamuses cool off in the calm waters of the Zambezi downriver from the falls.

as 90 per cent, but the Victoria Falls are never less than spectacular. The falls began to develop as a tourist destination around the turn of the 20th century, but recently they have become particularly well known for the number of adventure sports and activities available. These include helicopter flights over the falls, rafting on the whitewater rapids, and even bungee-jumping from the Victoria Falls Bridge. This road and rail bridge was commissioned by Cecil Rhodes and completed in 1905: according to Rhodes' specific instructions, the bridge (which he never saw) spans the Second Gorge so that the spray from the falls would land on the train carriages. Despite its age, the bridge remains an engineering marvel.

The Victoria Falls mark the frontier between Zimbabwe and Zambia, and both countries have created national parks in the area. A number of trails and viewing points have been established, and all manner of wildlife can be found in the environs. These include sizeable populations of elephant, buffalo, giraffe, zebra, antelope, hippopotamus and crocodile, and at least 39 species of birds of prey. The region's most spectacular wildlife is found downriver in the Lower Zambezi Valley National Park, between the Kariba Dam and the border with Mozambique. On the Zimbabwe side of the river, the Mana Pools National Park also shelters a huge wildlife population. Along this lush section of the Zambezi, visitors may be rewarded by a glimpse of the Cape clawless otter. Sadly, poaching and hunting wiped out the entire population of black rhino in the 1980s, but other animals, including antelope, zebra, wildebeest, lion and hyena, have thrived.

David Livingstone, the 19th-century explorer who was the first European to lay eyes on the falls, was so enraptured by the sight that he wrote 'scenes so lovely must have been gazed upon by angels in their flight'.

SAMARKAND

Latitude 39°39'N **Longitude** 66°57'E	
Location Central Uzbekistan	
Founded c. 700 BC	
Population 596,000	
Official language Uzbek, with numerous regional languages	
Currency The som	

Samarkand, legendary stopping point on the great Silk Road, is one of the oldest cities in the world. Established by the Persians in the seventh century BC, it became the centre of a vast empire under the rule of Timur (1336–1405), the powerful Mongol conqueror also known as Tamburlaine. He was almost as celebrated for his patronage of the arts as he was for his military prowess, and under his rule Samarkand was transformed into the greatest city in Central Asia. The finest craftsmen were summoned from across the empire to build splendid palaces and mausolea, madrassahs and mosques, which were sumptuously decorated with gold leaf, precious jewels and elaborate majolica tiles.

The heart of Samarkand's evocative old quarter is the Registan, flanked by three magnificent madrassahs (Islamic academies) covered with shimmering tile decoration. This was once the buzzing commercial and social centre of the city, with a caravansary for travellers, a huge covered market (the Chorsu trading dome still survives) and a shelter for wandering dervishes. Later, the Registan became the centre of the city's religious life. The Ulugbek Madrassah, completed in 1420, was the first of the trio of Islamic academies and was named for Timur's son. The Sher-Dor Madrassah (meaning 'having tigers') was erected between 1619 and 1636, and subtly echoes the design of the earlier building, but bears charming – and unusual – depictions of lions with tiger-like stripes and leaping gazelles on the main façade. A decade later, the Tilya-Kori Madrassah was commissioned: the name means 'gilded' and the turquoise dome of its mosque is lined with gold leaf.

The gigantic Bibi-Khanym mosque, just north of the Registan, is named for Timur's best-loved wife. The daring design

The focal point of Shah-i-Zinda, the extensive royal mausoleum complex, is the Mausoleum of Qasim-ibn-Abbas.

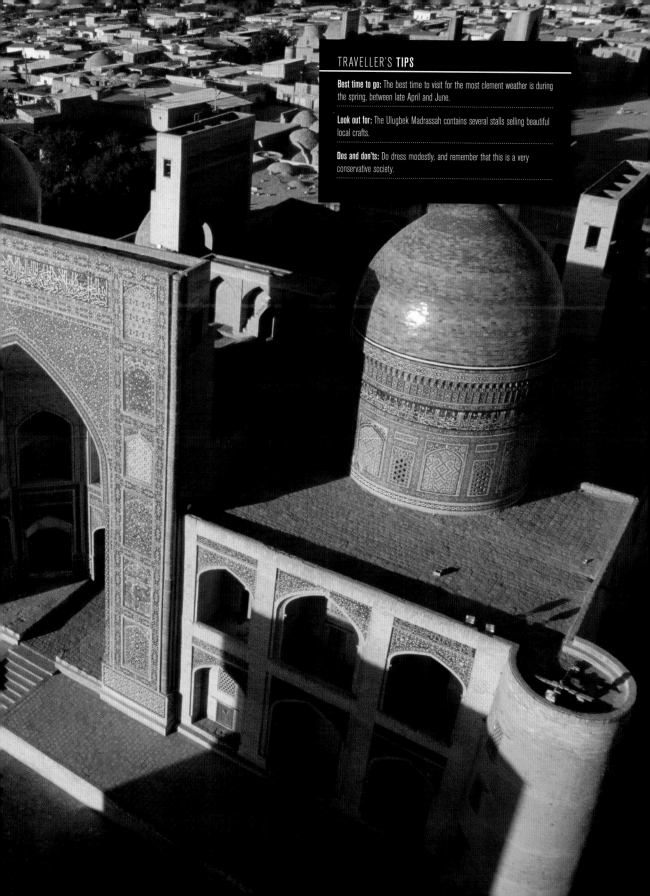

TRAVELLER'S **TIPS**

Best time to go: The best time to visit for the most clement weather is during the spring, between late April and June.

Look out for: The Ulugbek Madrassah contains several stalls selling beautiful local crafts.

Dos and don'ts: Do dress modestly, and remember that this is a very conservative society.

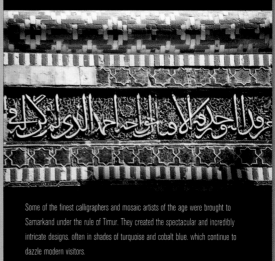

Some of the finest calligraphers and mosaic artists of the age were brought to Samarkand under the rule of Timur. They created the spectacular and incredibly intricate designs, often in shades of turquoise and cobalt blue, which continue to dazzle modern visitors.

incorporated thousands of precious jewels brought from Timur's military campaign in India. According to legend, the architect in charge of construction fell madly in love with the beautiful Bibi-Khanym and demanded a kiss. But when Timur heard of the exchange, he condemned the architect to death, and threw his adored wife off the highest point of the minaret. A bazaar sprawls chaotically around the foot of the mosque, where people of a dozen different ethnicities, speaking a babble of different languages and dialects, gather to buy cheese, vegetables and spices.

Timur is buried in the Gur-e Amir mausoleum along with several other members of his family. The massive domed mausoleum is all that survives of what was once an extensive complex of religious buildings, destroyed by earthquakes or invaders. Timur lies beneath an enormous slab of polished jade, which, according to legend, is inscribed with a threat of vengeance against anyone who disturbs the tomb.

Another royal mausoleum complex, Shah-i-Zinda, clings to a hilltop on the edge of the old city. It remains an important place of pilgrimage for local people, who believe that Qasim ibn-Abbas, cousin of the Prophet Mohammed, was buried here. He is commemorated in an eponymous mosque and madrassah at the heart of the complex. Most of the richly decorated tombs and mausolea were constructed in the 14th and 15th centuries, but the earliest parts of the complex date back to the ninth century AD. The best-preserved mausolea commemorate Timur's niece Shadi Mulk Aka and sister Shirin Bika Aka, and are covered in glittering tilework.

The 17th-century Tilya-Kori Madrassah is perhaps the most immediately recognizable building on Samarkand's most emblematic square, the Registan. Its enormous dome has become a landmark.

TAJ MAHAL

◇ Agra

INDIA

Latitude 27°10'N **Longitude** 78°02'E

Location Agra, India

Built 1632–1654

Materials Marble

Approximate area 3,000 square metres
(33,000 sq feet)

Approximate dimensions 55 x 55 x 35 metres
(180 x 160 x 115 ft)

The Taj Mahal is the most famous monument to love in the world. It was built, according to legend, by the Mogal ruler Shah Jahan in order to honour a death-bed promise to his wife Mumtaz Mahal (meaning 'Elect of the Palace'). She was betrothed to Shah Jahan at the age of 14 and would become his third and most beloved wife. She died giving birth to their 14th child in 1631, and he swore that he would build her a mausoleum without equal. Craftsmen from across the empire and beyond were summoned to Agra, capital of the Mogal empire, including calligraphers, sculptors, stonecutters and inlay artists, and the 28 different kinds of precious stones used in the construction came from as far afield as China and Arabia. It took 22 years, 20,000 workers and a convoy of 1,000 elephants to complete the sublime Taj Mahal, the crowning achievement of Mogal architecture.

A towering red sandstone wall protects the complex on three sides, with the river forming a watery barrier on the fourth. Entrance is through a magnificent gateway, with splendid arches and pale domes that subtly echo the great mausoleum itself. Several smaller tombs, built for consorts and valued servants, are scattered outside the gate. Within the walls is an extensive Persian-style garden, with raised parterres, fountains

At dusk, the Taj Mahal is a mass of violet shadows, the minarets, domes and cupolas of the mausoleum silhouetted against a deep-rose sky.

and reflecting pools. Originally designed to emulate the Gardens of Paradise, it was once filled with flowers and fruit trees, the ponds teemed with shimmering fish and exotic birds sang in the tree branches. Unfortunately, the gardens, which had fallen into neglect, were largely replaced with lawns and clipped shrubs by the British in the 19th century. However, the mausoleum is still reflected in a long, tranquil pool.

TAJ MAHAL

The tombs of Mumtaz Mahal (above) and Shah Jahan, formed by a square base topped with a casket, are elaborately inlaid with gorgeous jewels. Although the tomb of Shah Jahan is larger, that of Mumtaz Mahal sits at the exact centre of the mausoleum built in her honour.

The focal point of the Taj Mahal complex is, of course, the great, domed tomb itself. It is built of pale, luminescent marble, which shimmers as the light changes – glowing rose pink, pearl grey and soft yellow by turns. The vast dome, which is the tomb's most striking feature, is balanced on a square pedestal base, adorned on each side with a massive ornamental gateway, itself flanked with pairs of balconies. Symmetry, a fundamental tenet of Mogal architecture, is key to the Taj Mahal's design. A tall, slender minaret stands at each corner, ingeniously built to lean slightly outwards, so that, in the event of an earthquake, the minarets would not fall onto the tomb itself. The huge gateways and balconies are inlaid with polished jasper, jade and other gemstones, and the marble has been incised to create intricate abstract patterns. Calligraphy unfurls across the walls, using passages from the Qur'an, and stuccowork has been swirled into delicately formed flowers, plants and garlands.

The interior of the mausoleum is even more spectacular. Arches curve in symmetrical splendour around the lofty chamber walls, which shimmer with precious jewels and panels of calligraphy. The upper arches are adorned with viewing balconies, each with a delicately wrought screen of transluscent marble. A large octagonal screen, intricately worked into an ethereal garden of flowers, vines and leaves, surrounds the tombs of Mumtaz Mahal and Shah Jahan (the Shah was laid to rest beside his adored wife in 1666). Their bodies are buried below the tombs in the crypt, with their faces looking east towards Mecca in accordance with Muslim tradition.

The great domed mausoleum is reflected in a serene pool made of the palest marble. It is flanked by elegant, tree-lined avenues which provide a perfect perspective of the graceful edifice.

DARJEELING RAILWAY

Darjeeling

INDIA

Latitude 27°1'N **Longitude** 88°16'E

Location West Bengal, India

Built 1879–1881

Approximate dimensions 86 kilometres
(54 miles) long

Official languages Hindi and English

Currency Indian rupee

For more than a century, the Darjeeling Himalayan Railway has climbed up from the plains of West Bengal to the hill station of Darjeeling, high in the Himalayan foothills. It has been nicknamed the 'Toy Train', thanks to its narrow gauge (just 610 millimetres; 2 ft), but the little train manages the incredible feat of ascending 2,100 metres (6,888 ft) in less than 80 kilometres (50 miles). It twists its way up into the mountains on a spectacularly scenic 13-hour journey, passing jungle, tea plantations and rivers, with the stunning, snow-capped peaks of the Himalayan range providing a constant backdrop.

TRAVELLER'S TIPS

Best time to go: The best times are March–May or September–November. Summer temperatures can be extremely high.

Look out for: Tibetan prayer flags fluttering in the trees. This region has attracted numerous Tibetans who have fled their country.

Dos and don'ts: Do try some *chai* (hot, spiced tea) and snacks, sold by local women reaching in through the train windows.

Under the British Raj, Darjeeling was known as the 'Summer Capital', and provided Europeans with a cool retreat from the searing heat of the plains. From the mid-19th century, several large tea estates were established around the town, and the notion of a railway began to be mooted in order to reduce transport costs. Construction began in 1879 and was completed two years later. The steep gradient of the terrain posed unique engineering problems, which were ingeniously solved by the use of the very narrow gauge, and a series of reverses and sharp curves – some so extreme, that they actually loop back on themselves. Four extra loops and four zig-zagging reverses were added the year after the line opened when it was found that the locomotives were struggling with the gradient of the original line. After these initial problems were resolved, the line was a great success, and by 1910 it was carrying 170,000 passengers and nearly 50,000 tons of freight per year.

The Batasia Loop is one of the most dramatic, making a complete 360-degree turn. The obelisk within the loop is a war memorial.

Siliguri Town was the original starting point of the Darjeeling Himalayan Railway, although it was extended to New Jalpaiguri in 1964. As well as a pair of diesel engines, 12 original steam locomotives, built between 1889 and 1925, are still in use on the line, and add to the romance. The ascent is gradual at first, but becomes increasingly pronounced from Sukna, about ten kilometres (6 miles) from Siliguri. The flat plains give way to bamboo forest, rivers and glimpses of tea gardens. The first sharp curves begin about 15 kilometres (9 miles) into the journey: the spiral after Rungtong station is one of the most dramatic, curving like a figure-of-eight to accommodate the steep slopes. Most famous of all is Agony Point, the tightest loop of the journey, which gives breathless visitors the sensation of hanging over an abyss as the train turns tightly on a mountain spur. The views are exhilarating, stretching out across the valley below, with the striking peaks of the Bhutan Range to the east.

The highest point of the railway is reached at Ghum, which at 2,258 metres (7,406 ft) is the highest railway station in India, although it is still a good deal lower than the highest station in the world, Tanggula in Tibet, which is over 5,000 metres (16,400 ft) up. From Ghum, the train slips down to Darjeeling, set amid terraced tea gardens and backed by the distant silhouette of Mount Kangchenjunga.

The railway may be slow, but the gentle pace allows visitors to drink in the magnificent scenery. The splendid panorama of the Himalayas includes glimpses of the mighty peak of Mount Kangchenjunga – the third-highest mountain in the world.

The first tea plants in Darjeeling were sown in 1841. The plants flourished, and the British authorities decided to grow the crop commercially. Today there are 69 tea plantations in the region, covering an area of 200 square kilometres (77 sq miles) and employing about 50,000 workers, with almost double that number during harvesting.

ANGKOR WAT

CAMBODIA

◇ Angkor Wat

Latitude 13°26'N **Longitude** 103°50'E

Location Siem Reap, Cambodia

Built 12th century

Materials Sandstone and laterite

Approximate area Angkor Archaeological Park covers 400 square kilometres (150 sq miles)

Approximate dimensions Outer wall of temple is 3,600 metres (11,800 ft) long

The vast temple of Angkor Wat, the world's largest religious monument, emerges from thick forest in central Cambodia. It is the country's most beloved symbol, blazened on the national flag, and powerfully evokes the lost splendour of the Khmer civilization.

Angkor Wat is the largest and finest of the thousand or so surviving temples of Angkor, capital of the ancient Khmer empire from the 9th to the 15th centuries. Recent studies have concluded that Angkor was the largest pre-industrial city in the world, which may have supported a population of up to one million people. The jewel of this extraordinary city was the enormous temple of Angkor Wat. The scale is staggering: the central tower soars up for 200 metres (650 ft), more than twice the height of London's Big Ben, and the complex occupies a site so huge that it could accommodate the Vatican City 12 times over.

Angkor Wat was commissioned in the early 12th century by Suryavarman II (1113–c.1150) as his state temple and possibly his own mausoleum. Some decades after the death of Suryavarman II, Angkor was sacked by the Chams (from what is now southern Vietnam). It was repaired by the Emperor Srindravarman (1295–1308), who changed the state religion from Hinduism to Buddhism, converting Angkor Wat to a Buddhist temple.

TRAVELLER'S TIPS

Best time to go: Between December and March, when the weather is not too hot. To avoid the crowds, however, visit in November.

Look out for: At the end of the rainy season, in November and December, the pools are filled with beautiful lotus flowers.

Dos and don'ts: Do try to see Angkor Wat at sunrise or sunset. Do wear comfortable footwear: the complex is huge, with lots of steep steps to negotiate.

The great temple of Angkor Wat is a physical representation of Mount Meru, dwelling place of the Hindu gods. Access to the temple was progressively more exclusive: the common people were allowed only into the lowest level, while the upper level was for the king and priests.

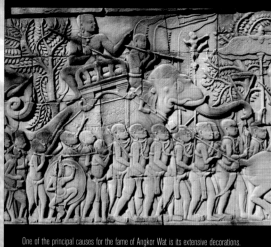

One of the principal causes for the fame of Angkor Wat is its extensive decorations, particularly the enormous bas-reliefs which have been incorporated into the architecture. These vividly depict myths and historical scenes, including the procession of Suryavarman II, which adorns the southern gallery.

Dedicated to Vishnu, the temple's design is a symbolic representation of the sacred mountain of Meru, abode of the Hindu gods and centre of the universe. The five towers on the highest level of the temple represent the peaks of the mountain of Meru, and the 190-metre-wide (623-ft) moat symbolizes the primordial ocean. The main entrance to the temple is via a causeway, which represents the rainbow that links the human world with that of the gods. Another raised causeway leads to the monumental gateway (*gopura*) at the entrance to the temple proper, topped with three huge pine-cone domes. The *gopura* is flanked by a vast statue of eight-armed Vishna, which was later converted into a statue of Buddha by the simple expedient of providing it with a new head.

A splendid colonnaded gallery encloses the third level of the temple, filled with the superb bas-reliefs for which Angkor Wat is justly famed. They still bear remnants of the scarlet and gold paint which would once have dazzled viewers, and illustrate rousing battles and other key events in Khmer history, scenes from daily life, and episodes from the Hindu epics the *Ramayana* and the *Mahabharata*. The 49-metre-long (160-ft) bas-relief which occupies much of the eastern gallery is the most famous piece of surviving ancient Khmer art. A sublime depiction of the Hindu creation myth, The Churning of the Sea of Milk, it features intricately carved *devas* (gods) and *asuras* (demons) churning the primordial ocean in order to release *amrita*, the elixir of immortality.

Angkor Wat is the most famous temple in the ancient Khmer capital, but it is just one of over a thousand to survive. One of the most beautiful is Ta Prohm, built by King Jayavarman VII as a monastery and university.

BOROBUDUR

Latitude 7°35'S **Longitude** 110°13'E

Location Jawa Tengah, Java, Indonesia

Built c. AD 750–850

Materials Lava stone

Approximate area 15,000 square metres (163,000 sq ft)

Approximate dimensions 123 x 123 metres (404 x 404 ft)

Borobudur is the world's largest Buddhist monument, a colossal pyramid-mountain set amid lush rice paddies in the centre of the Indonesian island of Java. Shaped like a mandala, it crowns a hilltop overlooking a sacred plain, and functions both as a physical representation of Buddhist cosmology, and a place of pilgrimage. The temple was founded around AD 750, during Southeast Asia's golden age of temple construction. The temple functioned only briefly as the island's spiritual centre, and was soon abandoned, perhaps after the eruption of nearby Mount Merapi. Borobudur lay forgotten for centuries before being rediscovered in 1814 by Sir Thomas Stamford Raffles.

Borobudur takes the form of a stepped pyramid, with six stacked rectangular storeys topped by three circular terraces and a central stupa forming the summit. The monument is divided into three sections: the lowest level symbolizes the Kamadhatu, which is the physical world, or the World of Desires; the second level is the Rupadhatu, the World of Form, a transitional sphere in which humans are released from their physical bodies; and the highest level represents the Arupadhatu, which is the World of Formlessness, the sphere of enlightenment. The whole structure is in the form of a lotus, the sacred flower of Buddha. Pilgrims follow a balustraded path that circles up the monument in a clockwise direction, tracing a meditative progress to the summit. The pilgrim's journey is aided by 1,460 beautifully carved reliefs, which

TRAVELLER'S TIPS

Best time to go: Between May and October (in winter there are heavy rains and high humidity, but fewer crowds). The weather is clearest in May.

Look out for: The view at sunrise. This is when the monument is at its most serene and inspiring.

Dos and don'ts: Do arrive as early as possible to avoid the crowds, which can become intense later in the day.

The immense stepped pyramid of Borobudur, a place of pilgrimage for Buddhists, lies at the centre of the island of Java.

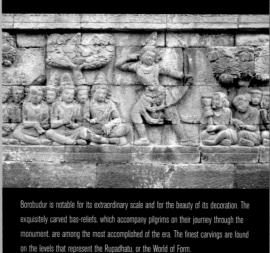

Borobudur is notable for its extraordinary scale and for the beauty of its decoration. The exquisitely carved bas-reliefs, which accompany pilgrims on their journey through the monument, are among the most accomplished of the era. The finest carvings are found on the levels that represent the Rupadhatu, or the World of Form.

depict scenes from the life of the Buddha and the principles of his teaching. The religious teachings are interspersed with episodes from everyday Javanese life and all kinds of folk tales and legends.

The pilgrim's journey begins in Kamadhatu, symbolized by the rectangular platform at the very base of the temple. This is the most richly decorated level, with some 160 carved panels depicting the joys and sadnesses which are experienced in the World of Desires, but most of the reliefs have been hidden by an extra wall, erected to provide support in the face of subsidence. The next five levels of terraces represent the World of Form, with 1,300 reliefs depicting scenes from the life of the Buddha and 43 bodhisattvas (enlightened beings), which instruct the pilgrim how to conquer desire and attachment. There are 432 Buddha statues at this level, seated in niches in the lotus position, which remind pilgrims of the object of their journey. The ornamention decreases progressively as the path continues to the summit, in a symbolic representation of the ascent towards the nirvanic state of nothingness.

As the path reaches the top, the balustrated corridors of the square galleries open out into the first circular terrace of the World of Formlessness. This terrace, and the two above it, are dotted with 72 perforated stupas (a dome-shaped symbol of enlightenment), each of which contains a statue of the Buddha meditating in bliss. At the centre of the highest terrace is a single stupa, which culminates in a gentle point, directing the viewer's gaze upwards towards heaven.

The upper terraces, which represent Arupadhatu (the World of Formlessness), are decorated with statues of the Buddha and several perforated stupas, one of the oldest Buddhist icons.

GREAT WALL

Latitude 40°21'N **Longitude** 116°00'E (Badaling)

Location Northern China

Built 221 BC–AD 1644

Materials Stone

Average height 5–9 metres (15–30 ft)

Approximate length About one third of the original 8,800-kilometre (5,500-mile) long network survives

The Great Wall of China is not one wall, but several, which were built between the eighth century BC and the 16th century AD to protect the northern borders of the Chinese empire. The network of walls, trenches and earthworks which comprise this mighty barrier constitutes the largest manmade structure in the world. Exhaustive new studies using the latest mapping technologies have revealed that it once stretched a staggering 8,800 kilometres (5,500 miles) across northern China. Although some sections of the Great Wall have long disappeared or crumbled into ruins, others have survived thrillingly intact.

The earliest defences were erected by warring factions in the northern reaches of what is now modern China. In 221 BC, these warring states were conquered by Qin Shi Huang, who unified the country and established the influential, but short-lived, Qin (pronounced 'Chin') dynasty after which China is named. Many of the walls that divided the former states were torn down, but those along the northern boundaries from Manchuria to Central Asia were consolidated in order to keep out tribes based in present-day Mongolia. Although patched under succeeding dynasties, little of the earliest stretches of wall have survived.

The final and most comprehensive period of construction took place under the Ming dynasty (1368–1644), considered the

TRAVELLER'S **TIPS**

Best time to go: The peak season is during spring and summer. Spring is always beautiful, but there are fewer crowds from late September.

Look out for: Try to visit some of the lesser-known and remoter parts of the wall for an authentic insight into its original function.

Dos and don'ts: Don't take home a piece of the wall as a souvenir, or add your name to the graffiti!

The Great Wall of China is not, contrary to popular myth, visible from the Moon. It is, however, the largest manmade structure on Earth.

greatest wall-builders in Chinese history. The huge network of defensive walls was renovated or rebuilt in an undertaking that took almost two centuries to complete. The walls crossed mountains and deserts, and work was hampered by bandits and wild animals. The work was so difficult and dangerous that it was said that a human life was lost for every foot of wall

completed. The Ming emperors deeply feared the Mongols, whose Yuan dynasty (established by Kublai Khan) had ruled the Chinese empire between 1271 and 1368 until being ousted by the Ming themselves. China was also increasingly harried by the Manchu, who periodically attacked the northeastern border from around 1600. The Ming walls were considerably higher than their precursors, and were heavily fortified. Armies were garrisoned at stages along the entire length of the network, canons were inserted at strategic points, and the walls were studded with double-storey watchtowers. The watchtowers were used to send messages between military posts, using smoke signals by day, and fire by night. Massive crenellations served both to protect soldiers from hostile fire, and to provide them with cover to attack invaders. These heavily fortified

walls have proved the most durable: almost all of the surviving stretches of the Great Wall that so entrance modern visitors were built during the Ming dynasty.

Peace, paradoxically, was not kind to the Great Wall. When the Manchu invaders finally took China in 1644, they established the Qing dynasty, which endured for almost 300 years. The Mongol territories were annexed, and, without the threat of northern invaders, the Great Wall fell out of use. Long stretches were dismantled, plundered for building materials or later bulldozed to make way for new roads.

Today, the Great Wall is under threat: desertification has swallowed up some sections, while others have been badly damaged by vandalism. How to protect the wall in a rapidly changing China remains an issue.

Several iconic stretches of the Great Wall have survived near Beijing, particularly around the tourist mecca of Badaling. These walls, with their sturdy guard towers and crenellations, snake apparently endlessly over the hills, and gave rise to the early misconception that first entrenched the notion that the Great Wall was a single entity.

FORBIDDEN CITY

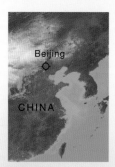

Beijing

CHINA

Latitude 39°54'N **Longitude** 116°23'E

Location Beijing, China

Built 1406–1420

Materials Wood, marble, bronze

Approximate area 720,000 square metres (7,750,000 sq ft)

Approximate dimensions 961 x 753 metres (3,150 x 2,470 ft)

The mysterious and beautiful Forbidden City is a vast imperial palace complex in the heart of Beijing. It has been home to 24 emperors since it was first built almost 500 years ago. Constructed under the Ming dynasty between 1406 and 1420, the Forbidden City remained China's political centre until the end of the Qing dynasty in 1912, when Puyi, the last Chinese emperor, was forced to abdicate. He and the imperial court remained in residence until 1924, when they were finally ousted and the Forbidden City was converted into the Palace Museum by the country's new rulers.

TRAVELLER'S TIPS

Best time to go: The best months to visit are May, September and October, when the weather is most temperate.

Look out for: The 1,400 elaborately carved dragons which double as water spouts, and create an enchanting spectacle on rainy days.

Dos and don'ts: Do arrive early to avoid the large tour groups. Don't miss the surprisingly small, but exquisitely beautiful, Imperial Garden.

Just 980 of the original 9,999 buildings have survived in the Forbidden City, but this nonetheless constitutes the world's largest group of preserved ancient wooden structures. The graceful halls now contain some superb artworks from the Ming and Qing dynasties. The vast complex was divided into two sections: the Outer Court, where the business of running the country was carried out; and the Inner Court, where the imperial family lived. The Forbidden City is spread over 720,000 square metres (7,750,000 sq ft), and is surrounded by a deep moat and an eight-metre-high (26-ft) wall. Its construction required more than a million workers, who filled it with rare and priceless materials. A splendid gate pierces the massive wall on each side, of which the grandest is the Meridian Gate on the south side, which is still the main entrance. There are five entrances in this gate, including the central archway through which only the emperor himself was allowed to pass.

The Forbidden City is surrounded by a broad moat. The vermillion pillars of the northwest tower are beautifully reflected in the tranquil waters.

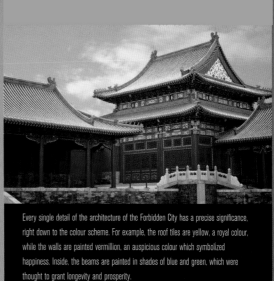

Every single detail of the architecture of the Forbidden City has a precise significance, right down to the colour scheme. For example, the roof tiles are yellow, a royal colour, while the walls are painted vermillion, an auspicious colour which symbolized happiness. Inside, the beams are painted in shades of blue and green, which were thought to grant longevity and prosperity.

Through the entrance are five exquisite bridges of white marble, which cross an undulating watercourse flanked with ornate balustrades. Water plays an important part in the Forbidden City's architecture: it serves not simply as a decorative device, but also has a protective function: fire was a constant threat in these wooden buildings. Beyond the watercourse is the Gate of Supreme Harmony, a fitting introduction to the Hall of Supreme Harmony that lies beyond it. This is the largest and most splendid of the palace buildings, the ceremonial heart of the Chinese empire. This is where the emperor was crowned, and where he held court from the gilded Dragon Throne. As the symbol of imperial power during the Ming and Qing dynasties, it was forbidden to erect any structure that was higher than this hall anywhere in the empire. The emperor used the nearby pavilion-style Hall of Central Harmony to confer with ministers and to rest before engagements. The Hall of Preserving Harmony completes the trio of buildings used for administrative purposes, and was used for official banquets. Behind it is a marble sculpture of a dragon with pearls which was so highly prized that anyone caught touching it was sentenced to death.

The Gate of Heavenly Purity, flanked by a pair of roaring lions in gilded bronze, marks the boundary between the Inner and Outer Courts. Beyond it lie the dwellings of the imperial household, including the Hall of Heavenly Purity, where the emperors slept. The Palace of Earthly Tranquility was the residence of the empress during the Ming dynasty. The smaller palaces and pavilions on the fringes of the Inner Court were used for the emperors' concubines and children.

Guardian lions, in bronze, marble or granite, guard the most important buildings. The lions are always in pairs, with the lioness playing with a cub (left), and the male lion standing with its paw on a ball.

KYOTO

JAPAN

◇
Kyoto

Latitude 35°41'N **Longitude** 139°45'E

Location Honshu, Japan

Population 1,466,000

Approximate area 828 square kilometres
(320 sq miles)

Official language Japanese

Currency The yen

Kyoto, the imperial capital of Japan for 11 centuries, is a
graceful city replete with exquisite palaces, temples, shrines
and gardens. Geisha, dressed in elaborate kimono, can be
glimpsed as they trip between the wooden teahouses of the
Gion quarter, and time-honoured festivals, such as the great
fire festival of Daimonji, take place much as they have for
centuries. But Kyoto is no museum city preserved in aspic:
the centuries-old architecture is set against a contemporary
backdrop of neon-lit skyscrapers and, although traditional
Japanese arts are prized and cultivated, the city also prides
itself on its dynamism and modern outlook.

TRAVELLER'S TIPS

Best time to go: The spring and autumn are beautiful seasons, thanks to the famous cherry blossom and colourful foliage, but Kyoto can be crowded.

Look out for: Wells (*chosuya*) at shrines. It is customary to wash your hands and mouth before entering a Shinto shrine.

Dos and don'ts: Do make a wish on a shrine tablet (*ema*): simply write your wish on the wooden tablet and add it to the collection.

平成十九年六月吉日建之

平成十七年二月吉日建之

平成十二年一月吉日建之

平成十五年十一月吉日建之

平成九年六月吉日建之

平成十八年二月吉日建之

Heian-Kyo, meaning 'Tranquility and Peace Capital', was established as seat of the Japanese imperial court in AD 794 and soon developed into the political, commercial and cultural centre of Japan. It was renamed Kyoto, 'Capital City', in the 11th century, and the arts, particularly poetry and literature, flourished. From the early 12th century, increasingly powerful feudal lords, protected by armies of samurai, began to jostle for supremacy. After the Minamoto clan defeated their rivals and assumed the title of Shogun for their leader, the imperial court fell into obscurity, and Japan was ruled by warriors for the next seven centuries. Kyoto was badly damaged during the civil wars which tore the country apart in the 15th century, and natural disasters – earthquakes and fire – also took their toll over succeeding centuries. However, its historic significance and beauty preserved it from the worst bombardments of the Second World War and it remains Japan's most beautifully preserved historic city.

Fushimi Inari-taisha is a Shinto shrine that is dedicated to the god of business. It is surrounded by woodland paths lined with red *torii*, traditional gates, dedicated by numerous Japanese businesses.

KYOTO

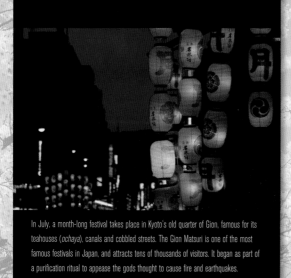

In July, a month-long festival takes place in Kyoto's old quarter of Gion, famous for its teahouses (*ochaya*), canals and cobbled streets. The Gion Matsuri is one of the most famous festivals in Japan, and attracts tens of thousands of visitors. It began as part of a purification ritual to appease the gods thought to cause fire and earthquakes.

Kyoto has preserved an impressive Imperial Palace, the latest of many to have occupied the site, which is still used by the Japanese imperial family. The current vast edifice, which saw the enthronement ceremonies of Emperors Taisho and Showa, was reconstructed in 1855 after it was destroyed by fire. The complex includes the graceful Sento gardens, all that survive of a small palace which burned down in the 19th century.

The city is packed with spectacular temples, shrines and gardens. One of the most emblematic sights is the enormous vermillion *torii* (the traditional gate found at Shinto shrines) at the Heian shrine (Heian Jingu), which was built in 1895 to commemorate the city's 1,100th anniversary. The shrine's design deliberately echoes that of the Imperial Palace. It is surrounded by exquisite gardens famous for their cherry blossom and the brilliance of the autumn leaves. The towering, five-tiered pagoda at Toji temple, rebuilt for the last time in 1643 but founded in the late eighth century AD, is the tallest wooden structure in Japan.

The dazzling Kinkakuji (Temple of the Golden Pavilion) is the city's most celebrated building, entirely covered with gold leaf, and reflected in a shimmering pool. The temple had survived unscathed by fire or war for five centuries before it was burned to the ground by a young monk with a history of mental instability in 1950. Now meticulously restored, it is the centrepiece of a gorgeous traditional Japanese garden, especially lovely in autumn. Ryoanji temple, built in 1450, is celebrated for its austerely beautiful Zen garden, with its carefully raked gravel patterns and precisely placed rocks.

The Kiyomizu temple is set amid cherry trees on a gentle hill overlooking the city. It was constructed, astonishingly, without the use of a single nail, and the views from its wide wooden verandah are justly renowned.

Gion is the traditional home of the city's geisha, known as *geiko* or *maiko* (a geisha apprentice). These women are highly trained entertainers, proficient in traditional music and dance, who attend their guests in exclusive teahouses. *Maiko*, with their elaborately painted faces, can occasionally be glimpsed on their way through Gion.

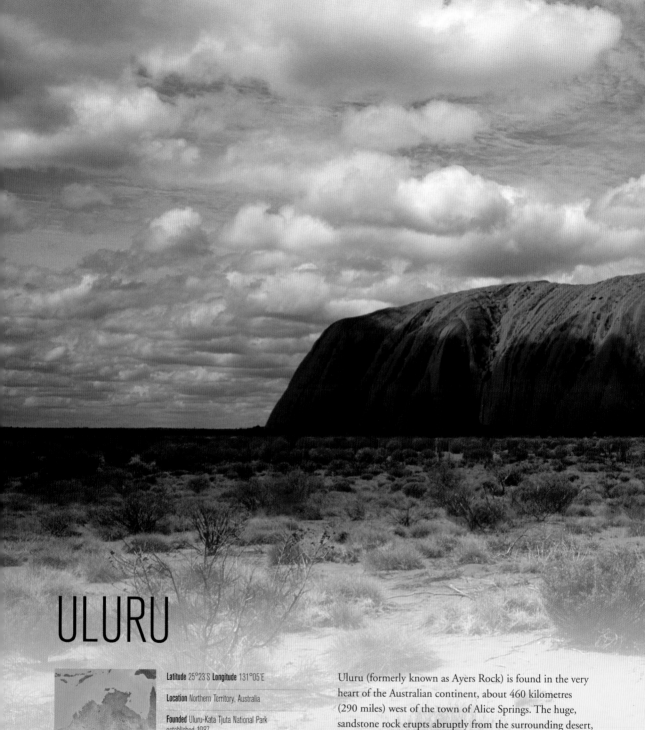

ULURU

AUSTRALIA

◇
Uluru

Latitude 25°23'S **Longitude** 131°05'E

Location Northern Territory, Australia

Founded Uluru-Kata Tjuta National Park
established 1987

Approximate area (National park) 1,325 square
kilometres (512 sq miles)

Approximate dimensions Uluru is 348 metres (1,141
ft) at its highest point

Uluru (formerly known as Ayers Rock) is found in the very
heart of the Australian continent, about 460 kilometres
(290 miles) west of the town of Alice Springs. The huge,
sandstone rock erupts abruptly from the surrounding desert,
the only surviving fragment of an ancient and long-
disappeared mountain range. The area around the rock has
been inhabited by the Anangu, indigenous Australians, for at
least 10,000 years. The giant rock, which they call Uluru, is a
sacred site to all Aboriginal Australians. At dusk, it glows a
deep, vibrant red, with the colours varying depending on the
changing light and the seasons.

TRAVELLER'S **TIPS**

Best time to go: Winter (April to October) is the best time to visit, with moderate temperatures and little rainfall.

Look out for: The most recently opened Talinguru Nyakunytjaku viewing area offers panoramic vistas, particularly at sunset.

Dos and don'ts: Do take a guided visit with a local ranger for a fascinating insight into the beliefs of Aboriginal Australians.

Uluru was first mapped by Europeans in 1873, when the rock was visited by William Gosse, a British surveyor. He named it Ayers Rock, after the then-Chief Secretary of South Australia, and it was known by this name until recently. Since 2002, it has been known officially as Uluru/Ayers Rock. Large swathes of Australia were declared as Aboriginal reserves in the first decades of the 20th century, including the region around Uluru, which was included in the South-Western Reserve. However, as the numbers of tourists increased, Uluru was sliced out from the reserve and the area was reclassified as the Ayers Rock-Mount Olga National Park (now the Uluru-Kata

Don't miss the great rock at sunset, when its colour gradually deepens from russet through a fiery red to a dusky violet.

Tjuta National Park). The land was returned to the Anangu in 1985, and is now managed jointly by the Traditional Owners and Australia's National Park Authority. The area that includes Uluru and the nearby Kata Tjuta mountains (which are also sacred to Anangu) has been inscribed on UNESCO's World Heritage List for its exceptional natural and cultural significance.

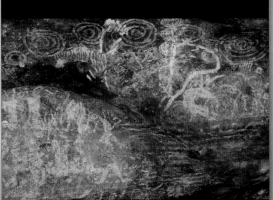

The Anangu have been documenting their creation stories and history with distinctive rock art at more than 90 sites around Uluru for thousands of years. Modern visitors can walk through the serene Kantju Gorge to see some beautiful examples of Anangu rock art, which is constantly refreshed according to local custom.

For the indigenous people of Australia, Uluru and Kata Tjuta are central to Tjukurpa, the traditional beliefs that govern every aspect of life. These sites are Tjukuritja, physical evidence of the time when the ancestral beings created the world. Tjukurpa is not written down, but transmitted from generation to generation through stories, songs, ceremonies and dances. Although some of this knowledge is secret and cannot be shared with non-Aboriginals, the Anangu are eager for visitors to learn as much of their traditional beliefs and customs as possible. Uluru and Kata Tjuta are surrounded by a network of walking paths, which allow for spectacular views of the beautiful rock and its shimmering palette of colours. The paths are also provided with information panels, which offer informative introductions to the local plants and animals and explain their uses for the Anangu. The best is the Uluru Base Walk, which encircles the rock: it also follows the route of Kuniya, an ancestral water-snake, to the Mutitjulu waterhole, which is just one of the creation stories connected with the rock. Local rangers offer fascinating guided walks, which offer a valuable insight into Tjukurpa.

The desert landscape around Uluru is full of distinctive flora and fauna, including a number of endemic plant species found nowhere else in the country. Reptiles thrive in this parched land, including the striking thorny devil, a colourful lizard covered in spines. Some species of wallaby and kangaroo may be seen, including the enormous red kangaroo, which can travel at 60 kilometres (38 miles) per hour. Bird life includes the magnificent wedge-tailed eagle, the brightly plumed crimson chat and the playful galah.

The desert landscape around Uluru and Kata Tjuta may appear arid and empty at first glance, but on closer inspection it teems with life. The area is home to numerous endemic species of animals, plants and birds.

GREAT
BARRIER REEF

Latitude 16°55'S **Longitude** 145°46'E

Location Queensland, Australia

Activities Diving, snorkelling, fishing, bird-watching, whale-watching, watersports

Approximate area (Great Barrier Reef Marine Park) 345,400 square kilometres (133,400 sq miles)

National language English

Currency Australian dollar

The Great Barrier Reef is the planet's largest coral reef system, composed of almost 3,000 individual reefs, which create a teeming underwater universe. It is located in the Coral Sea, just off the coast of Queensland in northeast Australia, and stretches for over 3,000 kilometres (1,900 miles). The Great Barrier Reef is one of the richest and most diverse ecosystems in the world, home to an extravagant variety of aquatic life, including turtles, dugongs (sea cows) and crocodiles. A large section of the reef is now protected as the Great Barrier Reef Marine Park, with countless different habitats that are home to numerous threatened and endangered species. The Great Barrier Reef is world-renowned for the outstanding opportunities it offers for outdoor activities, particularly snorkelling and diving, and attracts two million visitors annually.

Coral, contrary to popular belief, is not a plant but a tiny, living creature which is related to jellyfish and sea anemones. The individual corals (called 'polyps') create colonies by secreting a bony exoskeleton, which is then built on by other corals. It's slow work: a coral reef grows about 1.3 centimetres (0.5 in) each year (the Great Barrier Reef is thought to be about 500,000 years old). The Great Barrier Reef is not a single structure but a long chain of small reefs and islands: in the north, long ribbon reefs are more common, while the southern section has a liberal scattering of patch reefs interspersed with the low, sandy islands called cays. The reef ecosystems support a staggering array of marine life, including 400 different types of coral, 1,500 species of fish, and 6 species of sea turtle.

The Great Barrier Reef is the largest structure made by living organisms in the world. It is composed of a long chain of around 2,900 reefs.

The sharpfin barracuda is just one of the 1,500 fish species found in the teeming waters of the Great Barrier Reef. Barracudas are excellent hunters, preying on smaller fish with their long, fang-like teeth. They have an undeserved reputation for aggression, and almost never attack humans unless provoked.

One of the most entrancing creatures found around the reef is the manta ray. This is the largest species of ray and can grow up to seven metres (23 ft) wide. These are gentle creatures, which appear to delight in contact with humans, and often follow divers around the reef. They feed on plankton, krill and fish larvae.

The infinite colours and textures of this watery world are spellbinding, and attract divers and underwater enthusiasts from around the world. Shark attacks are virtually unheard of (despite the terrifying stories that circulate), and the most common species found here is the timid reef shark. Between June and October, whales and dolphins head up Australia's eastern coast on their way to their breeding grounds around the reef. The sea turtle is one of the highlights of any visit, paddling with surprisingly graceful movements between the reefs, and nesting on some of the glorious, white-sand beaches.

The sea turtle, like the lumbering dugong (sea cow), has particular significance for the indigenous Australians of this region. The Aboriginals and Torres Strait Islander people are the Traditional Owners of the Great Barrier Reef, and have occupied the region for more than 40,000 years. There are more than 70 clan groups living on or near the reef, which continues to play an important role in their beliefs.

The Great Barrier Reef stretches from near Fraser Island off the coast of Queensland to the Papua New Guinea coastline in the

north. The possibilities for diving and snorkelling on this vast strip are infinite, but the most popular base for visitors is Cairns (population 122,700). This large, modern city is well equipped for tourists, with a wide range of accommodation and diving companies on offer, and is only about one hour from the Great Barrier Reef. Port Douglas, about 70 kilometres (40 miles) north, is a much smaller community (population 3,000), but boasts some superb dive sites in the vicinity, including the Ribbon Reefs and several sites around Lizard Island. There are more than 600 islands in

A green sea turtle paddles among colourful fish such as the regal angelfish, moorish idol and dot and dash butterflyfish.

the Great Barrier Reef, all of which offer something different. Lady Elliott Island, at the southern end of the reef, is a paradise for nature lovers, with turtle nesting beaches and whale-watching, as well as wonderful diving. At the remote little island of Haggerstone, exploration of the delicate coral gardens is spiced with dives to historic shipwrecks.

GREAT BARRIER REEF

TASMANIAN WILDERNESS

AUSTRALIA

Tasmanian
Wilderness Area

Latitude 41°41'S **Longitude** 145°57'E

Location Southwest, west and central Tasmania

Founded Inscribed as World Heritage Area in 1982

National parks Cradle Mountain-Lake St Clair, Franklin-Gordon Wild Rivers, Hartz Mountains, Mole Creek Karst, Southwest, Walls of Jerusalem

Approximate area 13,800 square kilometres (5,300 sq miles)

The island of Tasmania contains one of the largest unspoilt stretches of wilderness in the world, with spectacular mountain peaks, ancient forests and numerous rivers, lakes and waterfalls. This pristine landscape has been recognized by UNESCO for its outstanding cultural and natural significance, and is protected as the Tasmanian Wilderness Area. It covers approximately 13,800 square kilometres (5,300 sq miles) and comprises six contiguous national parks. The most famous of these is the Cradle Mountain-Lake St Clair National Park, almost at the centre of Tasmania, which boasts jagged peaks and alpine meadows, as well as fantastic hiking trails.

TRAVELLER'S **TIPS**

Best time to go: The most popular time to visit is during the Tasmanian summer, between December and February. For the autumn foliage, visit in April.

Look out for: Tasmanian devils. These black marsupials are endangered, but the Cradle Mountain area has a substantial population.

Dos and don'ts: Do be prepared for very unpredictable weather. Don't feed the animals: this is strictly forbidden and those caught will be fined.

The Cradle Mountain region was one of the first to be protected in Tasmania, largely thanks to the efforts of an Austrian-born botanist called Gustav Weindorfer and his wife Kate. In 1912, they built a wooden chalet from the King Billy pine prominent in the park, and ardently campaigned for the establishment of a nature reserve. Their chalet, called Waldheim (Forest Home), remained in use as a guesthouse until the 1970s, when it burned down and was replaced by a modern copy. The wooden chalet is still a local landmark. Although a section was preserved as a scenic reserve in 1922, it was not until 1971 that the area became a national park.

Cradle Mountain and Lake Dove sit at the heart of one of Tasmania's most celebrated national parks.

Cradle Mountain and Dove Lake are the focus of numerous superb hikes, including a gentle, circular walk around the lake's perimeter, which passes through the enchanting Ballroom Forest, a temperate rainforest of silvery, lichen-covered trees. The most demanding walk is the celebrated Overland Track, a six-day hike through the magnificent mountain scenery at the heart of Tasmanian Wilderness Area.

TASMANIAN WILDERNESS

Cradle Mountain, at 1,545 metres (5,068 ft), is not the largest peak on Tasmania, but it is considered the most beautiful. Its craggy silhouette looms over the tranquil waters of Dove Lake, and its rocky flanks are criss-crossed with walking paths. The climb to the summit is rewarded with heart-stopping views, which stretch out in all directions.

The 65-kilometre-long (40-mile) route links Cradle Mountain with Lake St Clair, Australia's deepest lake, and can be extended by a series of side-trips to spectacular mountains, gorges and waterfalls. These side-trips might include a gentle stroll around Lake Will and a picnic overlooking the cascade of Innes Falls, or the stiff scramble up Mount Ossa, Tasmania's highest mountain at 1,617 metres (5,303 ft), to enjoy the impressive views. Other high points of this superb hike include the Acropolis, a stunning flat-topped peak said to resemble that of its Greek namesake, and the Labyrinth, which offers astounding views. The track is very well maintained, and the number of walkers is strictly controlled in order to ensure that its pristine beauty is preserved. It is famous for the constantly changing landscapes along the route, which include rocky peaks, wind-swept plateaus, temperate rainforest and flower-flecked meadows.

The Cradle Mountain region is renowned for its unique flora, particularly the pandani, a curious plant that resembles a palm tree, and the Fagus, a species of beech which has the distinction of being Australia's only deciduous tree and is endemic to Tasmania. The foliage is spectacular in autumn (April and May), when the leaves turn every shade from gold to the deepest red. Among the animals found within the park are some of the world's largest marsupials, including the endangered Tasmanian devil and two species of the cat-like quoll, as well as the elusive platypus and the echidna, which resembles a hedgehog. The park is also rich in bird life, which includes endemic species such as the Tasmanian thornbill, strong-billed honey-eater, black currawong and dusky robin.

The Southwest National Park protects swathes of pristine temperate rainforest. Although indigenous Tasmanians have hunted in this region for about 25,000 years, there is little evidence of permanent habitation.

TASMANIAN WILDERNESS

RAPA NUI

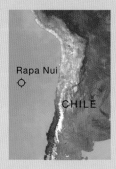

Latitude 27°9'S **Longitude** 109°26'W

Location Easter Island, Chile

Population 4,780

Approximate area 164 square kilometres (63 sq miles)

Official languages Spanish, Rap Nui

Currency Chilean peso

Easter Island, known to locals as Rapa Nui, is the world's most isolated inhabited island. A tiny triangular speck lost roughly midway between Chile and Tahiti in the Pacific Ocean, it has found worldwide fame thanks to the giant, enigmatic stone sculptures scattered across its landscape. There are almost a thousand of these huge figures, known as *moai* in the local language, which are believed to have been sculpted some time between AD 1000 and 1500.

The origins of the island's inhabitants are mysterious, although it is generally accepted that they are of Polynesian descent. The island and its people were given the Polynesian name of Rapa Nui – 'Big Rapa', after the Tahitian island of Rapa, which it was thought to resemble – in the 19th century. The earliest people on the island called their isolated home Te Pito o TeHenua, meaning 'The Navel of the World'. The most widely accepted theory among modern scientists and anthropologists is that a group of Polynesians arrived on the island some time between AD 400 and 800. According to local myth, Rapa Nui was settled by Hotu Matu'a (The Great Parent), who arrived in a pair of canoes with his wife, six sons and extended family, and became the first king (or *ariki*). According to oral myths recorded by the first missionaries to the island in the 19th century, the *ariki* was assumed to have god-like powers, and wielded absolute authority over the

TRAVELLER'S TIPS

Best time to go: Summer (January to March) is the most popular season, with warm weather and little rainfall. In winter, there will be fewer crowds.

Look out for: Tukuturi. This kneeling *moai* is unique on the island, and the only stone figure with legs.

Dos and don'ts: Do bring cash: credit cards are rarely accepted. Do try surfing, horseriding and swimming, which are all popular activities on the island.

Ahu Tahai is a ceremonial complex composed of three huge statues built on stone *ahus* (platforms). Sunset is a perfect time for photos.

islanders. The *ariki* was central to the cult of ancestor worship practised on the island, which gave rise to the celebrated *moai*.

Almost 900 of these massive stone figures have so far been discovered: just under half remain in Rano Raraku, which was the main *moai* quarry, but the rest are scattered across the island. Although they are often described as 'heads', in fact the statues depict complete bodies, although the heads are disproportionately large. The figures vary in size, but their stylized faces are curiously uniform. The red stone 'hats', whose function is still unknown, were added later. The *moai* represent the living faces (*aringa ora*) of deified ancestors, and almost all of them face inland across their clan lands. The only exceptions are the seven figures at Ahu Akivi, which gaze out across the ocean. It has been conjectured that they represent Hotu Matu'a and his six sons. The most important *moai* were erected on stone platforms, called *ahus*. All the statues are huge: the tallest completed statue is 10 metres (33 ft) tall, while one unfinished figure would have topped 20 metres (66 ft).

The Ahu Akivi site has seven uniform figures which, unlike every other *moai* on the island, face out across the Pacific Ocean.

The gigantic statues may have been transported from the quarry at Rano Raraku (above) to other parts of the island using a system of wooden sledges or rollers: although the island is now entirely deforested, wood was available until the mid-17th century, when the custom of building *moai* seems to have died out.

VANCOUVER

Latitude 49°25'N **Longitude** 123°1'W

Location British Columbia, Canada

Population 578,000

Approximate area 115 square kilometres (44 sq miles)

Official languages English and French

Currency Canadian dollar

Vancouver, Canada's third-largest city, occupies the beautiful Burrard Peninsula on the country's Pacific coast. The city is backed by the distant silhouette of the Canadian Rockies, and the surrounding coastline is pocked with inlets and coves. The presence of unspoilt landscapes so close to the modern city is what gives Vancouver its unique charm. In 1867, the city began in Gastown – a district that still preserves some of its historic buildings and cobblestoned streets – before being incorporated as Granville. It was renamed Vancouver in honour of the 18th-century British explorer in 1886.

TRAVELLER'S TIPS

Best time to go: Visit just outside the high summer season (May and June, or September and October) to avoid the crowds.

Look out for: Vancouver may not seem like an obvious beach destination, but it boasts some gorgeous strands right in the heart of the city.

Dos and don'ts: Do remember to tip – about 15 per cent is considered standard in restaurants. Do be prepared for cool evenings, even in summer.

The heart of modern Vancouver is Downtown, home to the financial district as well as most of the city's smartest shops, restaurants and hotels, and many of its most prestigious cultural institutions including the opera house. There are incredible 360-degree views out to the mountains and across the bay from the Vancouver Lookout, at the top of the slender Harbor Center Tower. Northwest of Downtown is Stanley Park, which, at 4,049 square kilometres (1,563 sq miles), is one of the largest city parks in North America. Its extensive forests and gardens provide a green lung in the heart of the city. Stanley Park is home to one of Vancouver's biggest attractions: the Aquarium Marine Science Centre, with its wonderful collection of aquatic creatures, including sea turtles, beluga whales, dolphins and sea otters. For those who want to see whales and dolpins in their natural habitat, Vancouver is a popular whale-watching destination between July and September.

Vancouver has a spectacular natural setting, backed by the massive peaks of the Rocky Mountains and overlooking the Straits of Georgia.

Eight totem poles stand next to an interpretation centre in one corner of Stanley Park. This exquisitely carved pole was made by Squamish artists, members of one of the First Nation peoples who have inhabited this stretch of coast for many centuries. The poles are carved from the trunks of large western red cedar trees.

Some of the best beaches in the city can be found in the vicinity of Downtown: these include Sunset Beach, English Bay (also known as First Beach), Second Beach and Third Beach. Vancouver is also ringed with stunning natural parks, including Lighthouse Park and Pacific Spirit Park in Western Vancouver. Lighthouse Park encompasses a huge swathe of virgin rainforest and is criss-crossed with walking trails. For garden lovers, the city is blessed with a number of exquisitely manicured botanical gardens, including the VanDusen Botanical Garden and Queen Elizabeth Park in South Vancouver, the Nitobe Japanese Garden, and the Botanical Garden at the University of British Columbia.

Popular day trips from the city include a visit to Vancouver Island and its capital Victoria. The years of British rule are recalled in Victoria's colonial-style mansions and English parks. The smaller islands in the Straits of Georgia are famous for their mild climate and the laid-back lifestyle of their inhabitants. The Gulf Islands National Park Reserve protects the islands' rich array of wildlife, which includes orcas, porpoises, sea lions, seals and otters.

Vancouver offers an enticing mix of big-city excitement and spectacular natural beauty. From Grouse Mountain, easily reached by gondola, there are thrilling views across the city from the ski slopes.

VANCOUVER

BANFF

Latitude 51°30'N **Longitude** 116°15'W

Location Alberta, Canada

Founded Banff National Park: 1885;
Jasper National Park: 1907

Visitor centres Banff, Lake Louise, Jasper

Approximate area Banff National Park: 6,641 square
kilometres (2,563 sq miles); Jasper National Park:
10,878 square kilometres (4,200 sq miles)

CANADA
◇
● Banff

The Canadian Rocky Mountains are among the world's great wilderness destinations. Much of this spectacular mountain range is protected in a series of national parks, of which the most famous are those of Banff and Jasper. These contiguous parks comprise a great swathe of Alberta's Rockies, and offer glorious mountain scenery, outstanding ski resorts, all manner of amenities for outdoor activities, and a stunning variety of local fauna – from grizzly bears to wolves.

Banff National Park was established in 1885, making it the oldest in Canada. It is enormous: 6,641 square kilometres (2,563 sq miles) of breathtaking peaks, glaciers, alpine meadows and forest, which together form a spellbinding mountain landscape. The main gateway to the park is Banff, the highest town in Canada, which developed as a tourist resort in the 1880s after a number of hot springs were discovered. The hot springs are still a big draw, but they have been joined by a host of other popular activities, including hiking, skiing, mountain biking, horseriding, dog sledding, ice-skating, ice-diving, golfing and canoeing. Although Banff is a popular year-round destination, there are two major ski resorts nearby – Sunshine Village and Ski Norquay – which offer outstanding facilities for winter sports. The national park offers more than 1,000 kilometres (600 miles) of walking trails, which encompass a stunning range of scenery.

TRAVELLER'S TIPS

Best time to go: The summer (July to September) is the best time for hiking and enjoying the scenery. The best months for skiing are February, March and April.

Look out for: Banff locals recommend Sunshine Meadows for its spectacular views of the highest peaks in the Canadian Rockies and flower-filled meadows.

Dos and don'ts: Do hike responsibly: visit the park information office for up-to-date weather reports and trail descriptions.

Moraine Lake's serene waters perfectly reflect the stunning snow-capped mountains, which circle the Valley of the Ten Peaks.

In addition, there are myriad opportunities for spotting animals and plants. The Vermilion Lakes area is probably the best for bird life.

Banff National Park is linked to the vast Jasper National Park to the north by the celebrated Icefields Parkway, a panoramic highway that stretches for 230 kilometres (140 miles) and cuts through a wild landscape of icefields, waterfalls and glaciers. It crosses the Columbia Icefield, the source of six enormous glaciers, and the largest glacial area south of the Arctic Circle and north of the equator.

Jasper is the largest national park in the Canadian Rockies, celebrated for the rich diversity of wildlife found within its borders, including moose, cougars, and grizzly and black bears. Although up to three million visitors a year visit Jasper National Park, it is always possible to find a pocket of

---

Bow Lake is a dazzling turquoise, and the colour intensifies from early summer. The lake, like many others within Banff National Park, is formed by glacial run-off, and its colour comes from the mineral-rich waters.

untouched wilderness. The park information office is located in the small community of Jasper, in an historic timber building dating back to 1914. The Whistler-Blackcomb ski resort, modernized for the 2010 Winter Olympics, is regularly voted among the best in the world, and there are numerous opportunities for crosscountry skiing. The entire park is well endowed with facilities for every imaginable outdoor activity, from fishing and horseback riding to rafting and even waterfall ice climbing. There are more than 1,200 kilometres (750 miles) of hiking trails and numerous spectacular mountain drives, such as the Mount Edith Cavell Road.

Ground squirrels, marmots, porcupines and elk (above) are commonly seen in Banff National Park, but it is also home to a number of grizzly and black bears. Among the 260 species of bird found within the national park are the bald eagle, osprey and rarities such as the American bittern, barred owl and pileated woodpecker.

CHURCHILL

Latitude 58°46'N **Longitude** 94°10'W

Location Manitoba, Canada

Population 900

Approximate area 54 square kilometres
(21 sq miles)

Official languages English and French

Currency Canadian dollar

Churchill, a small town of just under a thousand souls, is one of Canada's most remote communities. It sits on the banks of the Churchill River, just as it empties into the vast Hudson Bay in the far north of the province of Manitoba, and for most of the year it is a quiet port town. Every autumn, however, hundreds of polar bears descend on the town, where they wait for the waters to freeze over the bay, so that they can return to hunting seals, which are their primary source of food. It is estimated that as many as 1,000 polar bears congregate on the icy coastline around Churchill for a six-week period during

TRAVELLER'S **TIPS**

Best time to go: The polar bears descend on Churchill in October and early November. For whale-watching, the best time to visit is July and August.

Look out for: Fire-crackers – which sound alarmingly like gunshots – are used to keep polar bears safely out of Churchill.

Dos and don'ts: Do take a tour in a specially modified bus to see polar bears close up. Don't attempt to get within 100 metres (330 ft) of a bear while on

October and early November. The town proudly describes itself as the 'Polar Bear Capital of the World' and attracts as many as 10,000 visitors during the bear season, a short period of activity when tourists briefly outnumber the locals.

During winter, spring and early summer, the bears feed in the seal-rich waters of Hudson Bay. But, as summer progresses, the ice disintegrates, and the ice floes – with the bears on them – are nudged towards the southwest coast of Hudson Bay.

Here, the bears eke out a lean existence, eating seaweed, carrion and grasses, before heading north once again as the temperatures drop. The effects of global warming have made life even more difficult for the polar bears, which rely on ice to hunt. Their population has already dropped alarmingly, and the outlook is grim if present climatic conditions continue.

As many as 1,000 polar bears converge on the remote community of Churchill every autumn. They are waiting for Hudson Bay to freeze over.

The Arctic fox is common in the Churchill region and is usually easy to spot. Its fur changes from grey-brown when young to white once it reaches adulthood. The fox preys on lemmings, Arctic hare and even fish, and lives in large, complex dens that

The polar bears of Churchill are often surprisingly relaxed around visitors, who are taken out to the ice fields in tundra buggies. Some bears are shy, but others appear to relish the attention. Some bears are so curious that they will approach the tundra buggies at close range.

By October, the bears are hungry – and occasionally aggressive. Once, the polar bears were free to prowl through Churchill, but encounters with hungry bears led to the introduction of the so-called 'polar bear jail'. Animals caught within the town's perimeter are held here until the waters have frozen over and they can be safely released. Also, tourists can now view the bears up close from the safety of modified buses called tundra buggies.

Polar bears, the world's largest land carnivore, are the biggest draw for the ecotourists who descend on Churchill. But the town is also a wonderful place to spot beluga whales, which congregate in their thousands to calve in the warmer waters of the Churchill River during July and August. The huge pods of whales can be spotted – and their high-pitched twittering heard – from the shoreline, but several whale-watching cruises are also offered for those who want to admire these magnificent creatures at close range.

The region is also a paradise for bird-watchers, particularly during the spring and early summer, and a sizeable minority of the ecotourists come just for the bird life. More than 270 species have been spotted within a 40-kilometre (25-mile) radius of the town, including the snowy owl, tundra swan, American golden plover and gyrfalcon. The luckiest twitchers may be rewarded with a sight of the black-collared Ross's gull, among other rare species. More than 100 species of bird nest in the region, including the stilt sandpiper and Harris's sparrow.

The ghostly *aurora borealis* (Northern Lights) can be seen in late August and from December to April in the Churchill region. The lights, usually in hues of green or yellow, swirl across the immense northern skies.

MONUMENT VALLEY

UNITED
STATES
◇
Monument Valley

Latitude 36°58'N **Longitude** 110°06'W

Location Utah, United States

Materials Sandstone

Visitor centre Monument Valley Navajo Tribal Park
Visitor Center, off US Highway 163

Approximate area 5,000 square kilometres
(3,107 sq miles)

Entrance Off US Highway 163
(180 x 160 x 115 feet)

The blood-red landscape of Monument Valley, with its spires
and spurs, must be one of the most recognized panoramas
anywhere in the world. It has featured in hundreds of Western
movies, including John Ford's *Stagecoach* and Sergio Leone's
Once Upon a Time in the West, as well as television
programmes, adverts and music videos. The director John
Ford described it as 'the most complete, beautiful and peaceful
place on Earth'. Monument Valley lies entirely within the
Navajo Nation reservation on the Utah–Arizona border, and
is part of their homelands.

TRAVELLER'S TIPS

Best time to go: The best time to visit is May–June and September–October:
July and August are hot and crowded.

Look out for: Rock formations with evocative names bestowed by the Navajo,
including the Three Sisters, Sleeping Dragon and Ear of the Wind.

Dos and don'ts: Don't attempt to hike without a guide: this region is sacred
to the Navajo and they strictly limit access.

Although much reduced, the Navajo reservation is larger than several US states, and holds the country's largest tribe, with a population of about 250,000. The Navajo name for the valley is Tse' Bii' Ndzisgaii (Valley of the Rocks), and it remains home to Navajo families who have lived here for generations. The region is managed by the Monument Valley Navajo Tribal Park, who charge a small fee for use of the single road which makes a panoramic loop around the isolated valley. This 27-kilometre (17-mile) track of pounded dirt passes several of the startling spires, mesas and buttes which erupt from the flat, dusty land. The colours are saturated and intense, particularly at dusk and dawn, when the valley seems to glow hotly. Minerals – iron oxide for the red and magnesium oxide for the purplish-black – provide a prosaic explanation for the variegated hues of the iconic rocks, but the constantly changing light lends them an intangible magic.

The Navajo call the two enormous buttes at the entrance to Monument Valley 'the Mittens'. They are believed to fit the hands of the gods.

YELLOWSTONE

Latitude 44°36'N **Longitude** 110°30'W

Location Wyoming and Montana, United States

Founded 1872

Visitor centres Nine visitor centres and museums

Approximate area 8,983 square kilometres (3,468 sq miles)

Entrances Five entrances access the park from the north, northeast, east, south and west

Yellowstone National Park, established in 1872, is the oldest national park in North America. Set high on a lofty plateau and ringed with mountains, it is also one of the most geologically active regions in the world, with hundreds of bubbling hot springs and spouting geysers. This spectacularly varied and beautiful landscape encompasses vast tracts of open prairie, dense forest, dramatic canyons and almost 300 waterfalls, and is home to a wealth of wildlife, including grizzly and black bears, mountain lions, elk and American bison.

The national park boasts its very own Grand Canyon, gouged out over millennia by the Yellowstone River. It is 32 kilometres (20 miles) long and 275 metres (900 ft) deep. The canyon is located downriver of the magnificent Yellowstone Falls. These waterfalls, fringed with pine forest, are the biggest in the park. The Upper Falls are an imposing 33 metres (108 ft) high, but the Lower Falls plunge a massive 94 metres (308 ft) – twice the height of Niagara Falls. In spring, when the snow melts, they are especially breathtaking.

Yellowstone contains the greatest concentration of hot springs and fumaroles anywhere on Earth, and the legendary Old Faithful Geyser remains the park's most popular attraction. It is not the biggest or most powerful in the park, but, as the name suggests, it is among the most reliable, erupting

TRAVELLER'S TIPS

Best time to go: Try to visit in the shoulder seasons – June and September – to enjoy the park without crowds. Winter is beautiful but most roads are closed.

Look out for: The Lamar Valley is sometimes called 'America's Serengeti' because it attracts a huge concentration of wildlife.

Dos and don'ts: Do bring layers: temperatures can vary considerably within a single day. Do not approach any animals.

The steep-walled Grand Canyon of the Yellowstone is the largest of three canyons found within the park boundaries.

Eruptions of the Old Faithful Geyser usually last between 90 seconds and 5 minutes, and the column of steam shoots up between 40 and 55 metres (130–180 ft) in the air to the gasps of onlookers. In the 19th century, soldiers used the geyser as a laundry: garments placed in the crater just before eruption would emerge cleanly washed.

Yellowstone National Park contains the only continuously wild bison herd in the United States. The present herd, which numbers between 3,000 and 3,500, is descended from just 23 bison that survived the mass slaughter of the 1800s. Despite appearances, American bison are agile and extremely fast – and can easily outrun humans.

dramatically several times a day. Other reliable geysers in the Upper Geyser Basin include the Castle Geyser, Grand Geyser, Daisy Geyser and Riverside Geyser, linked by boardwalk trails. There are superb views over the basin from the top of Observation Point.

The prodigious Steamboat Geyser is the largest in the park – and the tallest geyser in the world. It is found in the Norris Geyser Basin, the hottest geyser basin in the region, a lunar landscape with steam hissing from cracked earth in a thousand hues. Steamboat's biggest eruptions shoot up more than 90 metres (295 ft) and are accompanied by an earth-shaking roar. Steamboat is notoriously erratic – intervals between recorded eruptions range from 4 days to 50 years. Nearby, a patch of small mudpot fumaroles edged with rainbow-coloured lava stone are nicknamed Artists' Paint Pots.

The pale, stepped terraces at Mammoth Hot Springs, near Fort Yellowstone, look like giant stepping stones tossed across a plain of striped volcanic stone. These limestone terraces erode quickly, changing the landscape ceaselessly. Fort Yellowstone, a collection of administrative buildings which now house the park authorities, was erected for the army who managed the park from its establishment to the founding of the National Park Service in 1904. The army instigated the construction of a road system, replacing the old waggon trails. The 225-kilometre-long (140-mile) road has been preserved and is called the Grand Loop Road Historic District. It provides a figure-of-eight loop around the main sights.

The Crested Pool is one of the most famous geothermal features of the Upper Geyser Basin. Its waters are a dark, peacock blue. Although the Crested Pool is a hot spring, it sometimes erupts like a geyser.

EVERGLADES

UNITED
STATES

Everglades

Latitude 25°50'N **Longitude** 81°00'W

Location Florida, United States

Founded 1947

Visitor centres Four visitor centres

Approximate area 11,700 square kilometres
(4,517 sq miles)

Entrances Four main entrances from the directions
of Homestead, Miami and Everglades City

The Everglades, poetically known as 'the River of Grass', is a
wide, slow-moving river of marsh and sawgrass covering some
11,700 square kilometres (4,517 sq miles). The river flows
gently from Lake Okeechobee towards the Gulf of Mexico
at the southern tip of Florida, and supports numerous
interdependent ecosystems, including cypress marshes and
mangrove forest. These are home to a wealth of wildlife
including several endangered species such as the leatherback
turtle and the Florida panther.

Until the last century, the Everglades had remained virtually
unchanged for thousands of years. The earliest signs of human
habitation date back 15,000 years, and the wetlands were
home to several Native American peoples for centuries until
the arrival of European explorers. Now, only a handful of
Native American communities remain in southern Florida.
Development of the region began only in the mid-19th
century when the notion of draining the Everglades was first
seriously raised. Over the last century, roads, factories and
urban sprawl have swallowed up half of southern Florida's
original wetland area, putting this unique watery landscape in
peril. The numbers of wading birds has been reduced by more
than 90 per cent, and dozens of other species are under threat.
The Everglades National Park was established in 1947 in order
to protect the landscape and its wildlife, but it covers just 20
per cent of the entire wetland area. Development outside the

TRAVELLER'S TIPS

Best time to go: The dry season (December–April), when there are fewer
mosquitoes and the lower water level means that animals gather around waterholes.

Look out for: More than 2,000 plant species that are found within the park
borders, including tropical ferns and waxy orchids.

Dos and don'ts: Do try the network of walking and biking trails, which lead
visitors through a variety of different ecosystems.

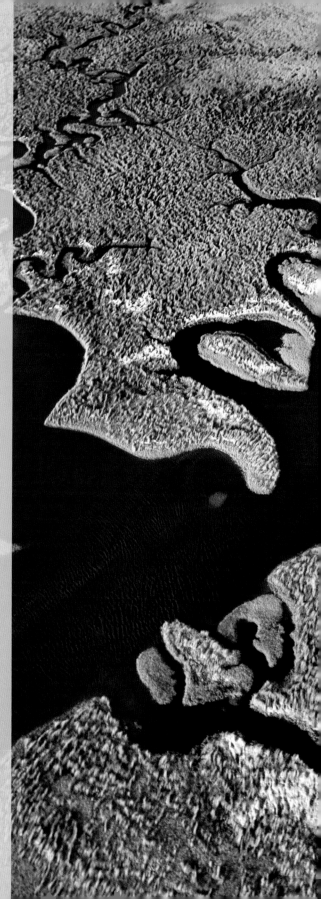

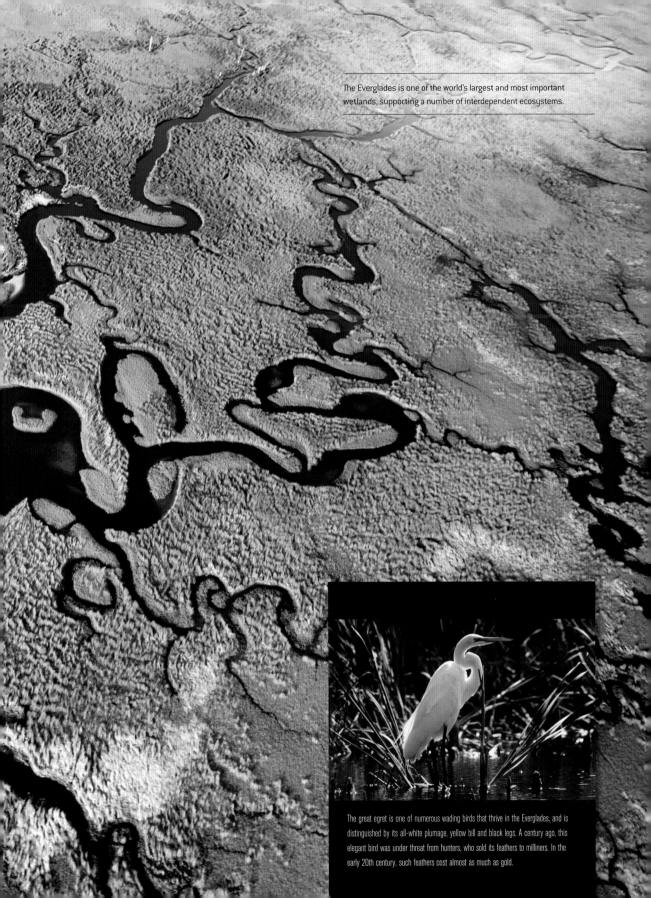

The Everglades is one of the world's largest and most important wetlands, supporting a number of interdependent ecosystems.

The great egret is one of numerous wading birds that thrive in the Everglades, and is distinguished by its all-white plumage, yellow bill and black legs. A century ago, this elegant bird was under threat from hunters, who sold its feathers to milliners. In the early 20th century, such feathers cost almost as much as gold.

South Florida is the only place in the world where crocodiles and alligators are known to co-exist, thanks to the confluence of brackish and saltwater habitats. Visitors may catch glimpses of the grey-green American crocodile, or the more common American alligator (above), distinguished by its creamy underbelly.

park boundaries continues to have an impact on the wetlands within, and the park authorities warn of its precarious state: 'The Everglades is on life support, alive but diminished.'

However, the national park continues to provide a refuge for more than 50 endangered species, including the American crocodile and the West Indian manatee. The filigree of waterways provide countless opportunities for visitors to encounter all kinds of spectacular flora and fauna at close quarters. Canoeing is the most evocative way to explore the Everglades: the park offers numerous canoe trails, which are well marked and suitable for all levels of proficiency. Among the most celebrated trails is the Wilderness Waterway, which takes around a week to paddle (the park authorities have erected camping platforms, called chickees, along the route). It's a predominantly estuarine area, where visitors may be rewarded with the sight of dolphins or manatees, or elegant wading birds such as roseate spoonbills and ibis.

Another superb canoe trail follows the Turner River, a wonderfully varied landscape which includes mangrove forests, sawgrass marshes and the fascinating tropical hardwood hammocks, which form curious 'tree islands' amid the low-lying sawgrass. All kinds of animals live in the hardwood hammocks, where the rich vegetation provides abundant food. These include white-tailed deer, bobcats, barred owls and marsh rabbits. More popular canoe trails can be found along the fringes of Florida Bay, where canoeists might see dolphins, sharks, sea turtles and even the occasional manatee.

The Everglades contains enormous mangrove forests, formed by three main species: red, white and black. Mangroves are well adapted to the zone of brackish water in the Everglades, where fresh and saltwater meet.

WASHINGTON MONUMENTS

Latitude 38°53'N **Longitude** 77°02'W

Location Washington, D.C., United States

Population 5,300,000 (metropolitan area)

Approximate area The city of Washington covers 177 square kilometres (68 sq miles)

Language The most widespread language in the United States is English, with Spanish second

Currency US dollar
(180 x 160 x 115 feet)

Capital of the United States of America since 1790, Washington, D.C. contains many of the country's most emblematic buildings and institutions. It provides a fittingly grand setting for more than a hundred monuments erected in memory of the soldiers and statesmen who devoted their lives to public service and the protection of their country. Many of these are illuminated at night, presenting a captivating panorama to visitors.

Several monuments are located on or around the National Mall, a ceremonial avenue fringed with some of the city's most celebrated museums and cultural institutions. It is overlooked at the western end by the Washington Monument, a tower shaped like an Egyptian obelisk and dedicated to George Washington (1732–99), first president of the United States. The vast column, reflected in a pool and surrounded by a park, has formed a distinctive part of the city's skyline since it was completed in 1884, and is still the world's tallest freestanding work of masonry. Visitors ascend in a glass-walled elevator to a special platform for a spectacular, birds'-eye view of all the city's landmarks, including the great dome of the Capitol building and the White House.

Another American founding father, Thomas Jefferson (1743–1826), is honoured with a circular neoclassical rotunda just south of the White House on the banks of the Potomac River. The cornerstone of the Jefferson Memorial was laid in 1939 by President Franklin D. Roosevelt, who had all the trees between it and the White House cut down so that he could see the memorial every morning. The interior of the rotunda is

The Jefferson Memorial is one of the most beautiful in Washington, D.C. An enormous bronze statue of the president dominates the interior, which is inscribed with many of his most famous writings.

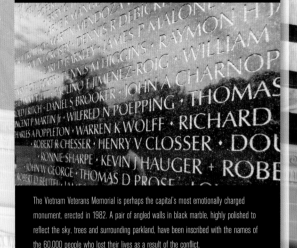

The Vietnam Veterans Memorial is perhaps the capital's most emotionally charged monument, erected in 1982. A pair of angled walls in black marble, highly polished to reflect the sky, trees and surrounding parkland, have been inscribed with the names of the 60,000 people who lost their lives as a result of the conflict.

inscribed with phrases from Jefferson's writings, and a bronze statue of the statesman stands next to an extended excerpt from his most famous work, the 1776 Declaration of Independence.

Jefferson's great admirer Franklin D. Roosevelt (1882–1945) is honoured in an expansive outdoor memorial which takes the form of four 'rooms', each representing a term in office. Sculptures and reliefs depict the 32nd president in representative scenes, including the 'fireside chat' radio broadcasts which he delivered during the 1930s, or waiting in a bread queue during the Great Depression. In one scene, he is accompanied by his beloved terrier, Fala, who was his permanent companion.

The Lincoln Memorial, dedicated to Abraham Lincoln (1809–65), takes the form of a Doric temple and is built of glistening white marble. It was designed by Henry Bacon and completed in 1922. A huge statue of Lincoln sits beneath the inscription 'In this temple as in the hearts of the people for whom he saved the Union, the memory of Abraham Lincoln is enshrined forever.' Lincoln steered his country through the Civil War, oversaw the abolition of slavery, and electrified the nation with the Gettysburg Address, one of the most celebrated speeches in history. The Lincoln Memorial has provided a symbolic setting for other famous discourses, including Martin Luther King's rousing 'I have a dream' speech, which he delivered to over 200,000 civil rights supporters from the steps of the Memorial in 1963.

Abraham Lincoln is honoured with a memorial in the form of a Doric temple. The design was loosely based on that of the Temple of Zeus in Olympia, Greece. The statue of the 16th president is six metres (20 ft) tall.

NEW ENGLAND

Latitude 42°21'N **Longitude** 71°03'W

Location Northeastern United States

States Maine, New Hampshire, Massachusetts, Vermont, Connecticut, Rhode Island

Main international airport Boston Logan Airport

Population 14,240,000

Approximate area 186,459 square kilometres (71,992 sq miles)

Nature puts on a ravishing spectacle every autumn in the beautiful forests of New England. From the end of September, the leaves turn myriad shades of red, gold, amber and russet, lit by the rays of autumnal sunshine. Six of America's oldest states make up New England – Connecticut, Maine, Massachusetts, New Hampshire, Rhode Island and Vermont – and many of the pretty towns and villages have a history that dates back to the 17th century and the first European settlements in the New World.

Most New Englanders live in Boston or along the busy coastline, but New England's hinterland, with its woods and mountains, villages and farms, rivers and waterfalls, is wonderfully empty and unspoilt. Much of the region is thickly covered with deciduous forests, which attract many visitors (locally called 'leaf peepers') in autumn. New England is famous for its country guesthouses and B&Bs, and the old-fashioned courtesy and slow pace of life make it the perfect weekend destination.

The region boasts several beautiful drives, including some nationally recognized Scenic Byways. One of the best is the Kancamuagus Highway, which cuts through the rugged White Mountains in central New Hampshire, and connects with the equally spectacular White Mountain Trail. The leaves are at their best between mid-September and mid-October in

TRAVELLER'S TIPS

Best time to go: The autumn colours peak between mid-September and mid-October in the north and between mid-October and mid-November in the south.

Look out for: In some parts of New England, moose regularly venture onto the roads, so watch out!

Dos and don'ts: Do book accommodation well in advance in autumn, as this is the most popular time of the year to visit.

The foliage of the sugar maple turns a glorious colour in autumn. It is highly prized in New England as a sap source for maple syrup.

The Slaughter House Bridge, which crosses Dog River in Vermont, was erected in 1872. It's a fine example of New England's covered wooden bridges, which were originally roofed in order to protect the heavy and expensive trusses (the largest wooden beams used in construction), thereby prolonging the bridge's life considerably.

this region. There are stunning, panoramic views over the forest and surrounding peaks from Loon Mountain, which can be reached via a gondola skyride.

In Connecticut, the Last Green Valley Byway (from Brooklyn to Lincoln) connects some of the region's oldest and most delightful towns. The autumn foliage makes a fine backdrop to colonial homesteads, meeting houses, churches and schools. The road also passes some of the distinctive covered wooden bridges which are such a feature of rural New England. In western Maine, the Rangeley Lakes Scenic Byway makes a breathtaking journey past lakes, forests, mountains and quaint villages. There are magnificent views from the celebrated viewpoint called Height of Land, which is justly considered one of the finest outlooks in all New England. This region is also particularly good for wildlife, and fortunate visitors will almost certainly see the stately moose which regularly appear on the roadside. Vermont's most famous drive is Route 100, which is a classic for admiring the autumn foliage. It passes the charming and historic town of Weston and the unspoilt wilderness of Gifford Woods.

The Contoocook River in New Hampshire is famously picturesque, its banks lined with hardwood forest which turns spectacular colours in autumn. The river is crossed by several charming bridges.

MEXICAN DAY OF THE DEAD

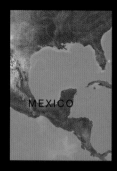

Latitude 19°25'N **Longitude** 99°07'W

Location Villages and towns throughout Mexico

Dates 1–2 November

Head for Pátzcuaro in Michoacán state

Official language Spanish, with 62 indigenous Amerindian languages

Currency Mexican peso

MEXICO

Each year, as October draws to a close, Mexicans begin to prepare for the Day of the Dead, El Día de los Muertos. It is believed that, on this day, the spirits of the dead can return to their homes and communicate with their loved ones. The markets are full of the bright blooms of *cempasúchitl* (marigold) flowers, which are used to decorate graves. Families prepare special foods, figurines and skulls made of sugar paste or chocolate to take to the graveside, and create colourfully decorated shrines to adorn their homes and welcome the spirits of the dead.

TRAVELLER'S TIPS

Best time to go: The Day of the Dead is held on 1 and 2 November, but the last fortnight of October is devoted to preparations for the event.

Look out for: *Pan de la Muerte* and other special foods. The 'bread of the dead' is traditionally placed at gravesides, with each region having its own recipe.

Dos and don'ts: Do feel free to walk through the cemeteries and admire the superb decorations, but don't pull out a camera without permission.

The Day of the Dead is a unique fusion of All Souls' Day – the Roman Catholic feast day introduced by Spanish colonial rulers – and 3,000-year-old customs bequeathed by the country's pre-colonial civilizations. Although El Día de los Muertos has been described as 'the cult of death', the Mexican feast is really a celebration of life. The indigenous people of Mexico believed that souls did not die, but went to Mictlán, a beautiful and peaceful place, where they could rest. Once a year, the spirits were able to visit their families, an event which, in pre-colonial times, took place for a whole month over July and August and marked the end of the indigenous year. The festivities were presided over by the goddess Mictecacíhuatl, known as the Dama de la Muerte (Lady of the Dead). It was a joyous and exultant event, a feeling that has been retained in the modern festival.

Many of the ancient rituals of Mexico's indigenous civilizations have been retained in some form or another in the modern celebration of the Day of the Dead. One of the key symbols of the festival is the skull, or *calavera*, made of sugar paste and

The *calavera* (skull) is the most popular symbol of the celebrations, and versions made of brightly coloured sugar paste are found everywhere. The *calavera* is also the name given to satiric political verses published in newspapers, which have become a modern tradition associated with the Day of the Dead.

decorated with bright swirls of icing. This has its roots in pre-Hispanic times, when families would keep the skulls of their dead loved-ones and display them as a happy reminder of life, death and the after-life. While in some cultures the skull is a symbol of fear, for the Mexicans it has no such association. Another popular reminder of ancient indigenous beliefs is La Catrina, a grinning female skeleton figure with a skull's head, which now presides over the celebrations just as the goddess Mictecacíhuatl once did. La Catrina, in her modern incarnation, owes her existence to an early engraving by José Guadalope Posada which appeared in 1913, and was popularized after the Mexican Revolution in the 1920s.

On 1 November, known as the Día de los Innocentes or the Día de los Angelitos (Day of the Innocents or the Little Angels), the children who have died are remembered, and masses of white flowers and candles are brought to their graves. Adults are commemorated during the main festival, which takes place the following day on All Soul's Day. Families head to the cemeteries, decorating the graves with bright, orange *cempasúchitl*, also known as the flower of a hundred petals or the flower of the dead. In Pátzcuaro, on the shores of Lake Pátzcuaro, northeast of Mexico City, locals celebrate the Day of the Dead by making delicate paper boats (called *mariposas*, meaning butterflies) and setting them afloat in a candlelit procession on the waters of the lake. Thousands of tourists descend on the city in droves in order to take part.

Cemeteries are turned into a riot of colour, with marigolds, said to resemble the rays of the Sun, the most commonly used flowers. Candles, photos, food and sometimes pillows and blankets are also placed on the graves.

CHICHÉN ITZÁ

Latitude 20°40'N **Longitude** 88°34'W

Location Yucatán peninsula, Mexico

International airport Cancun

Built AD 600–1000

Materials Limestone

Approximate area 15.5 square kilometres (6 sq miles)

MEXICO

Chichén Itzá

Chichén Itzá, a vast city of stone in northern Yucatán, Mexico, is one of the greatest achievements of the Maya civilization. Although it had risen to prominence by the seventh century AD, it reached the height of its power and influence throughout the 10th to the 12th centuries. Later abandoned, the complex was almost completely submerged in jungle by the time it was finally restored and excavated in the early 20th century. Excavation continues, but – for now at least – the great Maya city of Chichén Itzá still raises more questions than it answers.

TRAVELLER'S **TIPS**

Best time to go: A good time to visit is in winter: December is the most popular month, but come in November to avoid the crowds.

Look out for: The spectacular jaguar throne, once painted red and studded with jade, was discovered in the depths of El Castillo.

Dos and don'ts: Do arrive as early as possible to avoid the tour groups and to explore the site before the midday heat becomes excessive.

The Maya was among the most advanced and dynamic of the Mesoamerican civilizations. Elaborating on discoveries made by previous civilizations such as the Olmec, the Maya developed astronomy, calendrical systems and the only fully realized written language to emerge from the pre-Columbian Americas. They were skilled farmers, weavers, potters and builders. Famous for their huge, richly carved stepped temples, the Maya constructed these amazing buildings without the aid of metal tools, draught animals or even the wheel. Chichén Itzá embodies all the greatest advances of the Maya civilization, from its spectacular temples to its 'observatories' carefully aligned with the Sun and Moon.

The ancient Maya city sits amid the arid lowlands of the Yucatán peninsula. The region's few rivers run underground, and Chichén Itzá was built near two huge sinkholes, which

The stepped pyramid of El Castillo is dedicated to Kukulkan, the serpent god. It was aligned with astrological entities important to Maya culture.

Thanks to its unusual circular form, El Caracol (The Snail) is usually called 'the Observatory' in English. Although its original function is debated, most archaeologists agree that the building was constructed with specific astronomical functions. Its alignment reveals the Maya fascination with the planet Venus.

are called cenotes. These provided water year-round, but also played a part in Maya worship. The larger of the two, the Cenote Sagrado (Sacred Cenote), was used for sacrifice to the rain god, Chaak. Offerings including gold, jade and human bones have been discovered at the bottom of the water hole.

The centrepiece of Chichén Itzá is the enormous Temple of Kukulkan, popularly nicknamed El Castillo (The Castle) which, at 24 metres (79 ft), is the tallest structure on the site. It takes the form of a massive, four-sided pyramid and was built according to strict astronomical guidelines. There are 91 steps on each of the four sides, which, along with the platform at the summit, total 365 steps, or one for each day of the year. The temple is dedicated to Kukulkan, the plumed serpent, whose cult was the state religion of Chichén Itzá. A massive staircase in the middle of each side of the pyramid is adorned with a carved balustrade that culminates in a massive snake head with open jaws at the base. Every year, on the spring and autumn equinoxes (21 March and 22 September), a dark shadow is cast on the northern side that creates the illusion of a vast, feathered snake undulating down the staircase.

Near El Castillo is the Great Ball Court, a huge stone arena. Here the Maya played a popular ball game which featured human sacrifice – sculpted stone panels show gruesome scenes, including an unfortunate player being decapitated by the ball. The circular Observatory (called the Caracol, meaning 'snail' in Spanish) is another striking building. The Maya were extraordinary astronomers, tracking astrological events, cycles and the movements of Venus and Mars with great accuracy.

The Temple of the Warriors is adorned with a Chacmool, a type of reclining figure holding a basin. This is one of more than a dozen that have been found across the site, and is backed by columns depicting Maya warriors.

CHICHÉN ITZÁ

OLD HAVANA

Havana
CUBA

Latitude 23°8'N **Longitude** 82°23'W

Location Northwestern Cuba

Population (Havana) 2,500,000

Approximate area (Havana) 721 square kilometres
(278 sq miles)

Official language Spanish

Currency CUP (non-convertible Cuban peso) and CUC
(convertible Cuban peso)

La Habana Vieja – Old Havana – is the sultry heart of Cuba's
capital, an exotic, if down-at-heel, beauty which exudes an
infectious charm. The graceful Spanish colonial architecture
may be time-worn, but this unique city still hums with life
and colour. The occasional vintage Cadillac adds a little
Hollywood sparkle, a throwback to the days when the island
was a playground for American glitterati. A rhythmic
soundtrack to Old Havana's cinematic skyline is provided
by the omnipresent strains of Cuban music, wafting across
rooftops and echoing around every square.

Havana was established by Spanish conquistadors in 1515,
only two decades after Columbus made his journey of
'discovery' and claimed the Americas for Spain. Perfectly
placed on the burgeoning trade routes between the
Old and New Worlds, and blessed with a magnificent natural
harbour, the city soon flourished. But the dreams of gold
which brought floods of Spanish adventurers also enticed
pirates and corsairs, and the city came under constant attack.
In response, the Spanish fortified the city with walls, castles
and watchtowers, many of which – including the iconic
fortresses of El Morro and La Cabaña which guard the
harbour – survive today.

The Spanish ruled Cuba for almost four centuries, and
bequeathed the sumptuous Baroque mansions and churches,

TRAVELLER'S TIPS

Best time to go: April or early September, when the weather is not too hot and
there aren't too many crowds. Avoid hurricane season (mid-September to October).

Look out for: Che Guevara. Images of the iconic rebel leader are everywhere,
most famously on the exterior of the Ministry of the Interior building.

Dos and don'ts: Do make an effort to learn basic Spanish phrases: English is
not widely spoken. Do enjoy the city's atmospheric coffee houses.

The Plaza de la Catedral is dominated by its Baroque cathedral and fringed with handsome 18th-century mansions. The ensemble can be admired from the terraces of cafés scattered around the square.

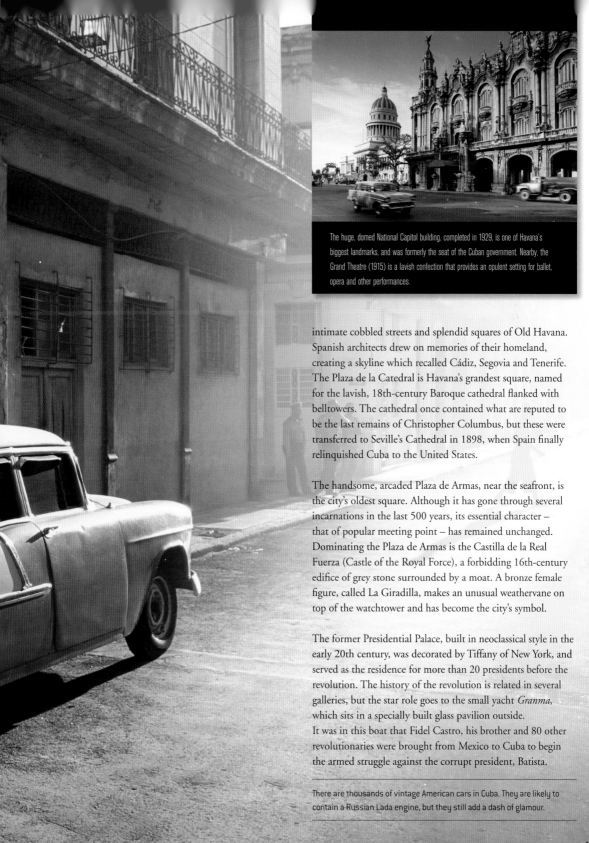

The huge, domed National Capitol building, completed in 1929, is one of Havana's biggest landmarks, and was formerly the seat of the Cuban government. Nearby, the Grand Theatre (1915) is a lavish confection that provides an opulent setting for ballet, opera and other performances.

intimate cobbled streets and splendid squares of Old Havana. Spanish architects drew on memories of their homeland, creating a skyline which recalled Cádiz, Segovia and Tenerife. The Plaza de la Catedral is Havana's grandest square, named for the lavish, 18th-century Baroque cathedral flanked with belltowers. The cathedral once contained what are reputed to be the last remains of Christopher Columbus, but these were transferred to Seville's Cathedral in 1898, when Spain finally relinquished Cuba to the United States.

The handsome, arcaded Plaza de Armas, near the seafront, is the city's oldest square. Although it has gone through several incarnations in the last 500 years, its essential character – that of popular meeting point – has remained unchanged. Dominating the Plaza de Armas is the Castilla de la Real Fuerza (Castle of the Royal Force), a forbidding 16th-century edifice of grey stone surrounded by a moat. A bronze female figure, called La Giradilla, makes an unusual weathervane on top of the watchtower and has become the city's symbol.

The former Presidential Palace, built in neoclassical style in the early 20th century, was decorated by Tiffany of New York, and served as the residence for more than 20 presidents before the revolution. The history of the revolution is related in several galleries, but the star role goes to the small yacht *Granma*, which sits in a specially built glass pavilion outside. It was in this boat that Fidel Castro, his brother and 80 other revolutionaries were brought from Mexico to Cuba to begin the armed struggle against the corrupt president, Batista.

There are thousands of vintage American cars in Cuba. They are likely to contain a Russian Lada engine, but they still add a dash of glamour.

COSTA RICAN CLOUD FOREST

Latitude 10°38'N **Longitude** 84°88'W

Location Monteverde Cloud Forest Preserve, San José, Costa Rica

Founded 1972

Visitor centre Signposted 6 kilometres (4 miles) southeast of Santa Elena

Approximate area 800 square kilometres (300 sq miles)

COSTA RICA

○ Monteverde

Cloud forests are very rare, evergreen forests found in tropical and subtropical mountainous regions of the world. The cooler temperatures cause clouds and mist to form, bringing a constant source of moisture to the forests and creating an incredibly lush and verdant landscape. This sustains an astonishing variety of plant, animal and bird life – including many species that are found nowhere else on Earth. Costa Rica is home to several expanses of cloud forest, notably the Reserva Biológica Bosque Nuboso Monteverde (Monteverde Cloud Forest Preserve) and the nearby Reserva Santa Elena.

TRAVELLER'S TIPS

Best time to go: During the dry season, between November and April, with December and January the most popular months.

Look out for: The resplendent quetzal is the symbol of the Monteverde preserve: although endangered, it is often sighted within the preserve's boundaries.

Dos and don'ts: Do reserve an entry pass for the Monteverde Cloud Forest Preserve in advance: visitor numbers are strictly limited.

The Monteverde Cloud Forest Preserve is private, but Costa Rica also boasts five national parks, which protect the superb cloud forests found across the country.

Costa Rica boasts greater biodiversity than the whole of Europe or North America, thanks to its wide range of habitats and its location at the cusp of tropical and temperate zones. The cloud forests have a crucial role to play in the country's biodiversity, by catching, storing and filtering the water that feeds into local communities. The relative humidity of cloud forest is often 100 per cent, perfect conditions for mosses, bromeliads, and the epiphytes (plants that grow, non-parasitically, on other plants), which flourish in moist environments. These act like sponges, soaking up the rainfall and releasing it slowly in the damp atmosphere.

Costa Rica is blessed with some of the most extensive cloud forests in the world. Several of these are protected by the state, while Monteverde is a private preserve. Its famous Sky Walk offers a series of dizzying suspension bridges with breathtaking views.

The keel-billed toucan is one of several species of toucan found in the Monteverde Cloud Forest Preserve. It is sometimes also called the rainbow-billed toucan for its enormous, brightly coloured beak, which is an extraordinarily adroit

The country's best-known nature reserve is the cloud forest at Monteverde, which straddles the Continental Divide and is home to an extraordinary wealth of plant, animal and bird life. There are more than 100 species of mammals, including 5 species of cats, over 400 species of birds, tens of thousands of insect species, and 2,500 species of plants, including more orchids than anywhere else in the country. The reserve currently attracts around 70,000 ecotourists a year, many of whom come hoping for a glimpse of the elusive resplendent quetzal, with its brilliantly coloured feathers. These large and incredibly beautiful birds inhabit the mountainous tropical forests of Central America; the species is currently under threat owing to the reduction of its habitat, but is most likely to be spotted during the nesting season (March to April). During the mating season, the male birds grow a spectacular train of tail feathers, which can be up to one metre (3 ft) long. The park contains 13 kilometres (8 miles) of easy trails near the most visited area by the park entrance, but more intrepid visitors can reach the wilds of the back country on remote and less accessible hiking trails.

On the fringes of the Monteverde reserve, tour operators have begun to provide alternative ways of viewing the cloud forest. The Sky Walk, a series of suspension bridges strung through

The Braulio Carrillo National Park, within reach of Costa Rica's capital, San José, holds one of the highest levels of biodiversity in the country, with 600 species of trees, over 530 species of birds, and 135 species of mammals catalogued so far. The park's dramatically varied altitude means that it offers ecosystems ranging from high-level cloud forest to tropical lowlands rainforest.

the forest (outside the protected reserve area), is one of the most popular visitor attractions, but others include a butterfly garden, and zip-line and canopy tours. A number of other tours are available, including night-time tours of the nature reserve, horseback riding and visits to the nearby Arenal volcano, one of the most active volcanoes in the world.

There are striking views of the Arenal volcano – smoking and belching lava – from the Santa Elena Reserve, which lies adjacent to Monteverde. Although Santa Elena is not as famous, or quite as richly endowed with plant and animal life, as its larger neighbour, its relative tranquility gives the reserve a particular charm. Among the many attractions of the Santa Elena area is the spectacular San Luís waterfall – at 100 metres (328 ft) high, this natural wonder is well worth a four-hour excursion through glorious cloud forest. The reward for the punishing hike is a glorious dip in the ice-cold pool at the foot of the waterfall.

Cloud forest, sometimes called fog forest, generally develops on the saddles of mountains, where moisture from cloud cover is retained. The forest is characterized by evergreens, with an abundance of mosses covering the ground like a carpet. Chancing upon waterfalls and their turquoise pools is one of the highlights of hiking through Monteverde.

GALÁPAGOS

Galápagos
Islands

ECUADOR

Latitude 0°40'S **Longitude** 90°33'W

Location Ecuador, 972 kilometres (608 miles) west of the mainland

Population 40,000

Approximate area 7,880 square kilometres (3,042 sq miles)

Official language Spanish

Currency US dollar

The Galápagos are a tiny sprinkling of volcanic islands in the Pacific Ocean about 970 kilometres (600 miles) west of mainland Ecuador. The archipelago comprises 13 main islands, 5 smaller islands, and 107 rocks and islets – all have been uninhabited for almost their entire history. They preserve an extraordinary number of endemic species – animals, birds and plants that are not found anywhere else on Earth. It was here, in this unique natural environment, that Charles Darwin began to formulate his theory of evolution by natural selection, which revolutionized scientific and philosophical beliefs. The islands have become known as a 'living laboratory for evolution', and remain extremely important for scientific research. In 1959, the entire archipelago was declared a national park, and the islands have become increasingly popular as an ecotourism destination since the 1960s.

The islands were first discovered by European explorers in 1535. They appeared on maps for the first time in 1570, when they were labelled Insulae de los Galopegos (Islands of the Tortoises). The magnificent, giant creatures that gave the Galápagos their name were almost wiped out in the 18th century. Whalers began to keep the tortoises on their ships as a food source, after discovering that the reptiles could go for months without food or water.

TRAVELLER'S TIPS

Best time to go: Avoid mid-December to January, and June to August, to escape the crowds. January to April are the best months for snorkelling.

Look out for: Lonesome George, the last Pinta Island giant tortoise, is kept at the Charles Darwin Research Centre.

Dos and don'ts: Don't attempt to explore the national park without a guide: the boundaries are strictly enforced. Don't approach or touch any wildlife.

The Isla de Santiago boasts a variety of landscapes, but perhaps most impressive is the Pan de Azúcar (Sugar Loaf) peak, climbed by Darwin. Expect to see Galápagos sea lions, marine iguanas, fur seals, land and sea turtles and an enormous variety of bird species.

The giant Galápagos tortoise, the largest tortoise in the world, remains the symbol of the islands, having been brought back from the brink of extinction. Once, about 250,000 of these lumbering creatures lived here, but that number has been reduced to 15,000. Of the original 15 subspecies, only 11 have survived.

The islands are one of the world's premier diving and snorkelling destinations. Two of the smallest and most remote islands – Wolf (Wenman) and Darwin (Culpepper) – are blessed with outstanding dive sites, some of the best places for experienced divers to see hammerhead sharks (above), whale sharks and manta and eagle rays.

In 1790, the first scientific expedition to the islands was undertaken, but the notes were lost and never found. On 15 September 1835, the HMS *Beagle* – a Royal Naval survey ship – arrived in the Galápagos. On board was Charles Darwin, a young naturalist who began to make extensive studies of the plants and wildlife found among the islands. These studies provided the basis for his theory of natural selection, presented in his groundbreaking book *On the Origin of Species*, which was published in 1859. This rocked the scientific world at the time, but has since become a fundamental tenet of modern biology.

The Galápagos Islands have changed dramatically in the last few decades. A century or so ago, they were virtually uninhabited, but now they support a population of around 40,000. Most of these settlers live on Santa Cruz, one of the larger islands. The islands now attract around 80,000 visitors a year. The national park authorities have managed to protect the landscape, thanks to stringently controlled access. Some islands are off limits to visitors, while others have visitor centres that allow tourists to experience the extraordinary diversity of the Galápagan flora and fauna. There are about 50 visitor centres dotted across the islands, carefully chosen to

showcase a variety of landscapes and habitats: those closest to Santa Cruz are the busiest, while the most remote are often the most interesting. Access to the national park's visitor centres is almost exclusively by boat, and the main settlements, particularly Puerto Ayora (the largest town and main tourist hub), offer a wide range of tours and cruises.

Santa Cruz is the headquarters of the Charles Darwin Research Foundation, established in 1959 to protect threatened, unique Galápagan species and their environment. They have implemented a breeding programme for the giant Galápagos tortoise. Another endemic species, the huge land iguana, has been similarly preserved. Española Island is particularly famous for its bird life, especially the endangered waved albatross and the blue-footed boobies who perform a curious mating dance in spring. The famous flightless cormorant, up to one metre (3.3 ft) tall, is found only on the islands of Fernandina and Isabela.

Darwin's finches, pictured here on the tail of a marine iguana, which developed slightly different characteristics depending on their location on the islands, were crucial to Charles Darwin's theory of evolution.

INCA TRAIL

Latitude 13°09'S **Longitude** 72°32'W

Location From near Cuzco to Machu Picchu, Peru

Options Classic Inca Trail begins 88 kilometres (55 miles) from Cuzco on the Urubamba River; Mollepata Inca Trail starts in the town of Mollepata; One-Day Inca Trail starts 104 kilometres (65 miles) along the railway from Cuzco to Aguas Calientes

Duration Three to four days for the Classic Inca Trail; five days for the Mollepata Inca Trail

The Inca empire was the largest in pre-Columbian America, comparable with the Roman empire in terms of its size and rigorous organization. Inca territories encompassed a 3,000-kilometre-long (1,900-mile) swathe of western South America, and a vast network of superb, paved roads linked the far-flung corners of the empire with the Inca capital at Cuzco. But, for all its size and accomplishments, the empire was shortlived. It rose to power in 1438 under the leader Pachacutec, who dramatically expanded Inca dominions; a century later, the Spanish conquistadors had taken Cuzco and set up a puppet government. They killed thousands of Inca, and forced many more into servitude in the gold and silver mines. Others died from imported diseases such as smallpox.

The Inca empire was wiped out, but Inca culture lives on in its historic heartland, high in the Peruvian Andes. Inca dress survives in the traditional costumes of the local people, and Inca language – Quechua – is still the most widely spoken indigenous language of the Americas. Although the Spanish destroyed the Inca capital at Cuzco, the vast network of stone-flagged mountain roads, tunnels and bridges was useful to the invaders, and was left largely untouched. Some of these paved roads are now incorporated into the Inca Trail, one of the most celebrated and spectacular hikes in the world. The four-day trail follows the breathtaking Urubamba Valley,

TRAVELLER'S TIPS

Best time to go: May is the best time to hike, with perfect weather, lush vegetation and few crowds. A section of the Inca Trail is closed in February.

Look out for: The Wiñay Wayna Inca ruins, on a remote cliff overlooking a terraced valley, are spectacularly beautiful.

Dos and don'ts: Do purchase your trail permit at least three months in advance. Do get in shape: the trail is arduous and altitude sickness can strike anyone.

Much of the Inca Trail is of original Inca construction. The Inca road system provided reliable routes for the empire's officials, messengers, soldiers, porters and llama caravans. Ordinary civilians needed permission before they could walk along these roads, while tolls were sometimes charged at bridges.

The spellbinding stone city of Machu Picchu is the climax of the Inca Trail, perched high on a ridge above the Urubamba Valley.

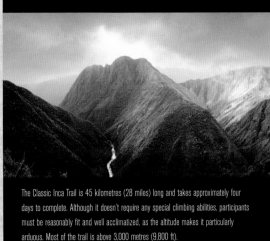

The Classic Inca Trail is 45 kilometres (28 miles) long and takes approximately four days to complete. Although it doesn't require any special climbing abilities, participants must be reasonably fit and well acclimatized, as the altitude makes it particularly arduous. Most of the trail is above 3,000 metres (9,800 ft).

crossing rivers and mountain passes, jungle and cloud forest, and passing the ruins of ancient Inca settlements. The highest point is the pass of Warmiwañusca (Dead Woman), at 4,200 metres (13,800 ft).

The culmination of the Inca Trail is Machu Picchu, a spellbinding city of stone perched above the Urubamba River. It is thought that as many as 1,000 people lived in the 200 or so dwellings which comprise the great city. Machu Picchu was begun in the mid-15th century under the great Inca leader Pachacutec, and abandoned – for reasons that remain mysterious – after the arrival of the Spanish. The vast Inca city, lost in clouds high on its mountain crag, was gradually forgotten, its location known only to locals for almost 400 years. The first foreigner to lay eyes on these magnificent ruins was the American explorer Hiram Bingham, who discovered Machu Picchu in 1911 while searching for Vilcabamba (capital of the breakaway Inca empire which was crushed in 1572). The discovery of the ruins caused great excitement, and the trickle of visitors soon became a flood.

The precise function of Machu Picchu remains obscure. Some have suggested that it was the winter palace of the Inca leaders – at 2,450 metres (8,036 ft), it is about 1,000 metres (3,300 ft) lower than Cuzco – while others believe that it was a fortress city guarding over trade routes. The most convincing theory is that it was a pilgrimage centre dedicated to Inca divinities. The most important buildings of Machu Picchu are found in the Sacred District, and include the Temple of the Sun, the Room of the Three Windows, and the Intihuatana.

The Inca stone masons of Machu Picchu were the finest the world has ever known, and it is said that their dry-stone walls fit so perfectly that not even a blade of grass can grow between the joins.

TIERRA DEL FUEGO

CHILE

ARGENTINA

Tierra del Fuego

Latitude 54°47'S **Longitude** 68°20'W

Location Shared between Chile and Argentina

Main cities Ushuaia (Argentina), Rio Grande (Argentina), Port Porvenir (Chile)

National parks Torres del Paine (Argentina), Tierra del Fuego (Argentina), Alberto do Agostini (Chile), Cabo de Hornos (Chile)

Approximate area 73,753 square kilometres (28,476 sq miles)

The Tierra del Fuego is an enormous archipelago of wild, windswept islands at the extreme southern tip of South America. The southern point of the archipelago forms Cape Horn. This region, right at the very end of the world, is cold and inhospitable: summer temperatures rarely top 9°C (48°F), and the thermometer hovers at around 0°C (32°F) for most of the winter. The coast is pocked with dramatic fjords and glaciers, and vast tracts of sub-Antarctic forest swathe the islands. The small communities that exist here are among the most southerly in the world.

The deep, narrow Garibaldi Fjord, in Chile, is embraced on either side by sheer cliffs, waterfalls and snow-covered mountain peaks. Ice bobs on the dark waters. At the head of the valley, the enormous Garibaldi Glacier spills into the icy sea. The glacier has been in retreat for most of the last decade, but has recently stabilized.

The earliest human settlement of the islands took place around 10,000 years ago, with the indigenous Yaghan being among the first peoples in the region. They were nomads, who travelled between the islands by canoe. Only one full-blooded Yaghan – also the last native speaker of the Yaghan language – survives today. The name Tierra del Fuego, which means 'Land of Fire', seems entirely inappropriate in this icy, barren land. It was bestowed on the region by the 16th-century Portuguese explorer Ferdinand Magellan, who glimpsed the fires of native peoples, and suspected that they were massing in

The magnificent Tierra del Fuego National Park incorporates the most southerly tract of the Andean Mountains. The peaks, valleys and forests stretch north from the Beagle Channel along the Chilean border, but are most easily accessed from Ushuaia, the Argentine regional capital.

the forests in order to ambush his armada. Tierra del Fuego was claimed by both Argentina and Chile, but was divided between the two countries in 1881. Chile now controls the western section, while Argentina contains the eastern part.

The guanaco is a nimble camelid native to South America, which thrives in the rugged wilds of the Tierra del Fuego. It stands about 90–120 centimetres (3–4 ft) tall and weighs around 90 kilograms (200 lb), and is russet or brown, shading to white underneath. Its wool, which is extremely soft, is highly prized. Llamas and alpacas are domesticated types of the guanaco.

In the last decades, the Tierra del Fuego has become increasingly popular as an ecotourism destination. The pristine landscape is imbued with a savage beauty, and supports a surprising amount of wildlife despite the harsh climate. Rural and sparsely populated, the islands offer a quiet tranquillity hard to find in the modern world. Fishing, trekking, sailing and horseriding are the most popular activities.

The lonely, wave-battered headland of Cape Horn overlooks an important sea link between the Pacific and Atlantic Oceans. Before the opening of the Panama Canal in 1914, these waters were continuously plied by clippers and other commercial ships, but the route was famously dangerous and difficult to navigate. Now, rounding 'the Horn' has become a significant yachting challenge, and the region has become a mecca for long-distance sailors.

The Alberto do Agostini National Park is a magnificent protected wilderness, so remote that some parts were only mapped during the 20th century. These rugged mountains and cliffs were sculpted by glaciers, including the celebrated Marinelli Glacier, with its 40-metre-high (130-ft) ice walls. Spectacular views of several awe-inspiring glaciers are afforded from the north shore of the Beagle Channel: this sailing route has become known as 'The Avenue of the Glaciers'.

The principal mountain range of the archipelago is known as the Cordillera Darwin, and stretches west–east across the Isla Grande de Tierra del Fuego, in Chilean territory. It is the continuation of the Patagonian Andes, and contains some beautiful and impressive peaks, particularly within the boundaries of the Alberto do Agostini National Park.

TRAVELLER'S **TIPS**

Best time to go: November to mid-March are the warmest and most popular months, but the archipelago offers year-round attractions.

Look out for: One of the most atmospheric accommodation options in the Tierra del Fuego is to stay on a working farm.

Dos and don'ts: Do take the End of the World steam train from Ushuaia to the borders of the Tierra del Fuego National Park.

PERITO MORENO GLACIER

ARGENTINA

Perito Moreno
Glacier

Latitude 46°36'S **Longitude** 70°55'W

Location Santa Cruz, Argentina

National park founded 1937

Nearest town Calafate

Approximate area Parque Nacional de los Glaciares covers 2,600 square kilometres (1,000 sq miles)

Approximate dimensions 30 kilometres (19 miles) long and 5 kilometres (3 miles) wide

The Perito Moreno Glacier is known as 'the White Giant'. Thirty kilometres (19 miles) long and five kilometres (3 miles) wide at its face, it is one of the largest and easily the most famous of the 365 glaciers found in Argentina's Parque Nacional de los Glaciares. This national park occupies about 2,600 square kilometres (1,000 sq miles), of which almost a third is under ice. These vast icefields contain 47 large glaciers: Upsala is the biggest, at about 50 kilometres (30 miles) long, but Perito Moreno is the most accessible. It is currently advancing at around seven centimetres (3 in) a year, making it

Best time to go: Between November and March, as this is when there is most activity on the glacier face.

Look out for: A number of tour operators in the nearby town of Calafate run special trekking trips on the glacier's massive flanks.

Dos and don'ts: Do explore the national park's other attractions, such as the arid Patagonia Steppe and the peaks of Mount Fitz Roy and Cerro Torre.

Thousands of visitors pour in daily to admire the glacier's enormous, blue-tinged face from the network of boardwalks laid out around the lake's edge – or from the boats that cruise the lake. Huge chunks of ice regularly break off with an ear-splitting boom, and plunge dramatically into the water below.

one of only two advancing glaciers in the Patagonian icefields – and one of very few in the entire world. Almost all the world's glaciers are in retreat, making Perito Moreno of interest to researchers investigating the effects of global warming.

The glacier rises majestically from the midnight-blue waters of Lago Argentino (Lake Argentine), the largest lake in the country, which is backed by the snow-capped peaks of the Andes. One of the most peculiar and celebrated features of the Perito Moreno Glacier is its propensity to advance across the lake

until it forms a massive icy wall or dam. The pressure of the water held back behind the glacial wall is immense, and eventually leads to a dramatic rupture accompanied by a thunderous roar so loud that it can be heard many kilometres away. This phenomenon is repeated in an unpredictable cycle of between three and seven years.

The Perito Moreno Glacier is named after Francisco Pascacio Moreno (1852–1919), an Argentine scientist ('*perito*' means expert in Spanish).

PERITO MORENO GLACIER

MANAUS AND THE AMAZON

Latitude 03°06'S **Longitude** 60°01'W

Location Amazonas, Brazil

Approximate area (Amazon rainforest) 8,235,430 square kilometres (3,179,717 sq miles)

Approximate length of River Amazon 6,400 kilometres (4,000 miles)

Official language Portuguese, with Spanish and numerous indigenous languages also spoken

The Amazon rainforest is the largest in the world, so huge that it contains within its depths indigenous peoples who have never seen a white face, and more species of plant and animal than anywhere else in the world. The vast canopy is fed by the biggest river on Earth, the Amazon, which holds one fifth of the world's freshwater. The region has become an increasingly popular destination for ecotourism in the last decades, and the Amazonian port-city of Manaus is the main hub for Amazon river cruises.

Manaus was founded by the Portuguese in 1669, who used it as a base for the trade in so-called 'red gold' – slaves. Although the slave trade remained important, it was rubber that really made Manaus' fortune during the 19th century. The finest surviving buildings in the city's small historic quarter date from this period, and include the world-famous Teatro Amazonas, and the Palàcio da Justiça, which is said to have been modelled on the palace of Versailles. Gustave Eiffel designed the Mercado Municipal, where all manner of exotic fruit and vegetables, fish and meat are piled high under an elegant wrought-iron canopy.

TRAVELLER'S TIPS

Best time to go: Peak periods for travel to Manaus and the Amazon are July to September.

Look out for: The Amazon is home to a threatened species of freshwater dolphin: the Amazon river dolphin.

Dos and don'ts: Do bring a hammock, sun block, mosquito repellent, water, snacks and toilet paper when travelling by river boat.

The Anavilhanas Archipelago in the Rio Negro, about 100 kilometres (60 miles) upstream from Manaus, is the largest freshwater island system in the world. It offers great opportunities for wildlife watching.

The Belle Epoque Teatro Amazonas is a splendid opera house located in Manaus. It is topped with a sumptuous tiled dome, made with imported German tiles, and the plush interior is a whirl of gilt, marble and velvet. The stage curtain depicts the meeting of the Amazon's two main tributaries, the Rio Negro and the Solimões.

The pale-throated, three-toed sloth lives in the canopy of the Brazilian rainforest. It can hang on to trees so securely with its hooked claws that it is known to sleep while seeming to dangle precariously above the forest floor. Although slow in the trees, the three-toed sloth is an adept swimmer.

Manaus sits at the confluence of the Rio Negro and the Rio Solimões, which together form the Amazon. One of the most popular river trips is to the Encontro das Águas (Meeting of the Waters), about 15 kilometres (9 miles) downstream, in which the dark, espresso-coloured waters of the Negro join and flow alongside the milky waters of the Solimões. From Manaus' Punta Flotante, the river ships pick up passengers for the journey upriver to the depths of the rainforest. More adventurous travellers may take one of the traditional two-storey river boats. Fortunate visitors may be afforded a glimpse of river dolphins or caiman and be given the chance to fish for piranhas. Several local tour-operators offer lodge-based tours in the region: the lodges farthest from Manaus usually offer the best chance to see wildlife.

The *Victoria amazonica* water lily is native to the shallow waters of the Amazon Basin. Its leaves, up to three metres (10 ft) in diameter, float on the water surface.

MANAUS AND THE AMAZON

IGUAÇU FALLS

Latitude 25°41'S **Longitude** 54°26'W

Location Brazil–Argentina border

River Iguaçu River

Approximate dimensions 2.7 kilometres (1.7 miles) wide

Official languages Portuguese (Brazil), Spanish (Argentina)

Currencies Brazilian real and Argentine peso

The fifth-largest waterfall in the world, and arguably the most spectacular, the Iguaçu Falls (Foz do Iguaçu in Portuguese, and Cataratas del Iguazú in Spanish) straddle the border between the Brazilian state of Paraná and the Argentine province of Misiones. Unlike other famous waterfalls such as the Victoria Falls, Iguaçu is not formed by one continuous curtain of water, but by 275 thunderous cataracts plunging in a spectacular 2.7-kilometre-wide (1.7-mile) strip. There are walkways and platforms on both sides of the falls that allow for a variety of different viewpoints, including one spectacular mirador that

TRAVELLER'S TIPS

Best time to go: December and Easter can get very busy. The rainy season (December to March) is when the falls are at their peak flow.

Look out for: Moonlight tours are one of the most romantic ways to see the falls.

Dos and don'ts: Do come prepared for unpredictable weather, with layers of clothing and waterproofs (which are provided at some visitor centres).

showcases a glorious 260-degree arc of waterfalls. All but three of the largest falls are on the Argentinian side, but Brazil counters with some of the most picturesque scenery.

The falls' name comes from an indigenous Guarani or Tupi phrase meaning 'great water'. Local myth tells of a powerful god in the shape of a huge serpent, who fell in love with a beautiful girl called Naipi and wanted to marry her. But she fled with her lover Tarobá in a canoe, enraging the god, who struck the river and created a tremendous gorge and waterfall.

It is said that Naipi was turned into a rock, beaten by the waters for all eternity, while Tarobá was turned into a palm tree leaning over the edge of the cliff. The first European to lay eyes on the falls was the Spanish explorer Álvar Núñez Cabeza de Vaca, who saw them in 1541 (the scene was memorably re-created in the film *The Mission*). One of the waterfalls on

The Iguaçu Falls, broken up by islands and ledges to form almost 300 separate cataracts, can be viewed from both Brazil and Argentina.

The waterfalls form the centrepiece of two national parks, one in Brazil and another in Argentina. These were created to protect the subtropical jungle around the falls, and the flora and fauna within it. Among the endangered species to be found in the region are the spotted jaguar (above) and the purple-breasted parrot.

the Argentine side now bears his name. The falls were virtually forgotten until the 19th century, when they were rediscovered and became an increasingly popular tourist attraction. Now the falls are one of the most visited sights in South America.

The most dramatic of the cataracts at Iguaçu Falls is the Devil's Throat (Garganta do Diabo in Portuguese, Garganta del Diablo in Spanish), which plunges into a canyon with such power that it is usually obscured by a 30-metre (100-ft) cloud of spray, filled with rainbows. The horseshoe-shaped waterfall is 82 metres (269 ft) high and 150 metres (492 ft) wide, and gives the dazzled visitor the impression of water plunging on all sides. The sound is deafening: this is the world's mightiest single waterfall in terms of volume, with up to 6,500 cubic metres (229,500 cu ft) of water per second thundering down into the canyon below. The best views of the Devil's Throat are had from a viewing platform at the end of a long wooden walkway on the Brazilian side of the falls. For an exhilarating, close-up view, take a walk along the trails which span the river feeding the falls on the Argentine side: expect to get soaked with spray (waterproofs are provided). Other notable falls are the Salto San Martin, Salto Bossetti and Bernabe Mendez. One of the most exciting ways to see some of these waterfalls is by boat: there are jet boat tours available from both sides of the falls. True adrenaline junkies might consider rappeling, which involves being lowered by rope down a cliff-face.

For panoramic views of the Iguaçu Falls, it's best to visit the Brazilian side (left). The Argentine side has an excellent network of trails and boardwalks, which allow visitors to get close to some of the most dramatic cataracts.

HAUKADALUR

Latitude 64°18'N **Longitude** 20°17'W

Location Southern Iceland

Population (Iceland) 320,000

Number of geysers in Iceland Around 800

Official language Icelandic, with English and Danish widely spoken

Currency Icelandic króna

ICELAND
Haukadalur

Iceland is – geologically speaking – one of the youngest and most volatile countries in the world. Glaciers inch across its frozen surface, while volcanoes thunder and bubble in the fiery depths. This collision of fire and ice has created a spectacular, otherworldly landscape, where snow-flecked plains give way to steaming geothermal pools, and geysers jet boiling water high into the sky.

The Haukadalur valley in southern Iceland is pocked with fumaroles – volcanic vents that smoke quietly in the crisp air, occasionally hissing a slim column of steam and gas. This region is famously home to the Great Geyser, the oldest erupting hot spring in the world, which was first described in the 13th century. It has given its name to the phenomenon (geyser, from the Icelandic verb 'to gush') and, at its peak, was jetting columns of steam up to 60 metres (197 ft) in the air. The Great Geyser remained very active until the early 1900s, when it suddenly became dormant. In 2000, it was jarred awake by a bout of subterranean volcanic activity, and now erupts erratically, usually once or twice a day. Fortunately for the thousands of visitors who make the trek to this remote geothermal zone, the nearby Strokkur Geyser can always be relied on to put on an explosive show. This usually occurs every five to ten minutes, and Strokkur can emit jets of steam that reach 30 metres (98 ft) in the air.

Strokkur (which means 'the churn') is Iceland's most reliable, active geyser. On the very coldest days, the steam turns into ice when it hits the ground in a theatrical natural feat.

TRAVELLER'S **TIPS**

Best time to go: Iceland has something to offer year-round: the white nights draw summer visitors, while festivals and winter sports draw tourists in winter.

Look out for: Wallow in a naturally heated pool, surrounded by volcanic landscape, at the Blue Lagoon, about 45 kilometres (28 miles) from Reykjavik.

Dos and don'ts: Do try delicacies such as *hákarl* (putrefied shark), washed down with a shot of ice-cold Brennivin (liquor made from potatoes and caraway).

INDEX

A

Aboriginal Australians 104–7, 110
Accademia, Venice 49
Africa 66–71
Alexander Column, St Petersburg 55
Alhambra 14–17
Amazon rainforest 7, 180–83
Amboise, Château d' 29
Amesbury Archer 12
Andes 6, 7, 170, 175, 176, 179
Angkor Wat 6, 84–7
Arenal volcano 165
Argentina 175, 178–9, 184–7
Aswan, Egypt 6, 62–5
aurora borealis 40, 130
Australia 104–11
Ayers Rock 7, 104–7
Azay-le-Rideau, Château d' 29

B

Bacon, Henry 144
Banff National Park 124–7
Barcelona 6, 18–21
Bastille, Paris 32
Bavaria 38–9
Beijing 95, 96–9
Belgium: Bruges 34–7
Bertholet, Gilles 29
Bingham, Hiram 173
Blois, Château de 29
Bofill, Ricardo 18
Bohier, Thomas 29
Borobudur 6, 88–91
Braulio Carrillo National Park 164
Brazil 180–87
Bruges 6, 34–7
Buddhism 6, 84, 86, 88–91
Burckhardt, Johann Ludwig 58

C

Cairns 111
Cambodia: Angkor Wat 84–7
Canada: Banff 120–31
Cape Horn 174, 176
Cappadocia 56–7
Carter, Howard 65
Castro, Fidel 161

Catalunya, Spain 18
Catherine the Great 55
Chambord, Château de 26–7
Charles VIII of France 29
Charles d'Orléans 29
Chenonceau, Château de 28–9
Chichén Itzá, Mexico 7, 154–7
China 7, 92–9
Churchill, Canada 7, 128–31
cloud forest 7, 162–5, 173
Colosseum, Rome 6, 42, 45
Columbus, Christopher 158, 161
Connecticut, USA 148
coral reefs 108–11
Costa Rica: cloud forest 7, 162–5
Cradle Mountain, Tasmania 112–15
Cuba: Old Havana 6, 158–61
Cuzco, Peru 170

D

Darjeeling Railway 7, 80–83
Darwin, Charles 7, 166–9
Day of the Dead, Mexico 150–53
Derinkuyu, Turkey 57
Diane de Poitiers 29
diving 108, 168

E

Easter Island 6, 116–19
ecotourism 164, 166, 176, 180
Egypt 6, 7, 62–5
Eiffel Tower, Paris 30, 32
Elephant Island, Aswan 62
England: Stonehenge 10–13
Everglades 7, 138–41

F

fairy chimneys 56–7
Ferdinand and Isabella 17, 20
Forbidden City, Beijing 96–9
Forum, Rome 42, 43
France 7, 22–33
François I of France 26–9, 30

G

Galápagos Islands 7, 166–9
gardens 77, 102, 123

Garibaldi Fjord, Chile 175
Gassend, Pierre 40
Gaudí, Antoni 6, 18, 19, 20
Germany: Neuschwanstein 38–9
geysers 134–7, 188–9
Giant's Causeway 7, 8–9
glaciers 176, 178–9, 188
Göreme, Turkey 56, 57
Gosse, William 105
Granada, Spain 14–17
Great Barrier Reef 7, 108–11
Great Meteoron, Thessaly 50
Great Wall of China 7, 92–5
Greece: Metéora 50–51

H I

Hammerfest 40–41
Haukadalur, Iceland 188–9
Haussman, Baron Georges 33
Havana 6, 158–61
Hermitage, St Petersburg 55
Hinduism 6, 84–7
Hittites 56–7
Hoarusib Canyon, Namibia 66
Hudson Bay 7, 128–9
Iceland 7, 188–9
Iguaçu Falls 7, 184–7
Inca Trail 6, 7, 170–73
India 76–83
Indonesia 6, 88–91
Italy 42–9

J K

Japan: Kyoto 7, 100–103
Jasper National Park 126–7
Java: Borobudur 6, 88–91
Jefferson Memorial 142–4
Jordan: Petra 58–61
Karnak, Temple of 65
Khmer empire 6, 84, 86
Kom Ombo, Temple of 62–5
Kyoto 7, 100–103

L

Leonardo da Vinci 26, 29, 30, 32
Lincoln Memorial 144–5
Livingstone, Dr David 68, 71

Loire Valley 6, 26–9
Louis XII of France 29
Louvre, Paris 30–32
Ludwig II of Bavaria 38–9
Luxor, Egypt 62–5

M
Machu Picchu 6, 7, 170–73
Magellan, Ferdinand 175
Maine, USA 148
Manaus, Brazil 180–83
Manchu 94–5
Mary Queen of Scots 29
Maya 7, 154–7
Medici, Catherine of 29
Metéora 50–51
Mexico 150–7
Michelangelo 45
Ming dynasty 93–5, 96, 97, 99
moai 116–19
Mont-St-Michel 7, 22–5
Monteverde Cloud Forest 162–5
Montmartre, Paris 30–31, 32
Monument Valley 132–3
Mumtaz Mahal 76, 79

N O
Nabateans 58
Namibia 7, 66–7
Nasrid dynasty 14
Native Americans 132–3, 138
Navajo Nation reservation 132–3
Neuschwanstein 38–9
New England 146–9
New Hampshire, USA 146, 148
Nicholas II, Tsar 54
Nile River 6, 7, 62–5
Northern Ireland 7, 8–9
Northern Lights 7, 40, 130
Norway: Hammerfest 40–41
Notre Dame, Paris 30, 32–3
Nouvel, Jean 18
Overland Track, Tasmania 7, 113–15

P Q
Pacific Islands 116–19
Palazzo Ducale, Venice 47, 49

Pantheon, Rome 6, 45
Paris 30–33
Perito Moreno Glacier 7, 178–9
Peter and Paul Fortress 54
Peter the Great 52–3, 54
Petra, Jordan 6, 58–61
Philippe II of France 23
plants 107, 115, 163, 164, 183
polar bears 7, 128–30
Port Douglas 111
Qasim ibn-Abbas 75
Qin Shi Huang 92
Qing dynasty 95, 96, 97, 99

R
Raffles, Sir Thomas Stamford 88
railways 7, 80–83
rainforest 69, 115, 123, 180–83
Ramesses II, Pharaoh 65
Rapa Nui (Easter Island) 6, 116–19
Rhodes, Cecil 71
Roaring Dunes, Namibia 66
Rockies, Canadian 120, 121, 124–7
Romans 61
Rome 6, 42–5
Roosevelt, Franklin D. 142, 144
Russia: St Petersburg 53–5

S
Sagrada Família, Barcelona 18, 20
St Mark's, Venice 47–9
St Peter's, Rome 45
St Petersburg 53–5
Samarkand 7, 72–5
Santa Elena Reserve 162, 165
Shah Jahan 76, 79
Shintoism 101
Sistine Chapel 45
Skeleton Coast 7, 66–7
Spain 14–21
Stonehenge 6, 10–13
Strokkur Geyser, Iceland 188–9
Suryavarman II 84, 86

T
Taj Mahal 76–9
Tasmania 7, 112–15

Thebes, Egypt 6, 65
Tierra del Fuego 6, 174–7
Timur (Tamburlaine) 72–5
Titus, Roman Emperor 42
Trezzini, Domenico 54
Turkey: Cappadocia 56–7
Tutankhamun, Pharaoh 65

U V
Uluru (Ayers Rock) 7, 104–7
UNESCO World Heritage Sites 6, 7, 8, 23, 52, 56, 105, 112
USA 132–49
Uzbekistan: Samarkand 72–5
Valley of the Kings/Queens 65
Van Eyck, Jan 37
Vancouver 6, 120–23
Vatican City 45
Venice 6, 46–9
Vermont, USA 148
Victoria Falls 7, 68–71
Vietnam Veterans Memorial 144

W Y Z
Wagner, Richard 39
Washington, D.C. 142–5
Washington, George 142
Weindorfer, Gustav and Kate 113
whale watching 121, 130
White Mountain Trail, USA 146–7
wildlife: Africa 66, 71
    Australasia 107, 115
    cloud forest 163–4
    coral reef 108–11
    Everglades 138–41
    Galápagos Islands 166–9
    marine 66, 121, 123
    North America 126, 127, 128–30, 134, 137, 148
    rainforest 183
    South America 176, 187
Winter Palace, St Petersburg 54–5
Yellowstone National Park 7, 134–7
Zambezi River 7, 68–71

METRO BOOKS
New York

An Imprint of Sterling Publishing
387 Park Avenue South
New York, NY 10016

Created for Quercus by Tall Tree Books Ltd

Managing editor: David John
Designer: Sandra Perry
Indexer: Christine Bernstein

ISBN: 978-1-4351-5165-9